A WISCONSIN BOY IN DIXIE

CIVIL WAR LETTERS OF JAMES K. NEWTON

A WISCONSIN BOY
IN DIXIE

CIVIL WAR LETTERS

OF JAMES K. NEWTON

EDITED BY STEPHEN E. AMBROSE

THE UNIVERSITY OF WISCONSIN PRESS

A NORTH COAST BOOK

The University of Wisconsin Press
114 North Murray Street
Madison, Wisconsin 53715

3 Henrietta Street
London WC2E 8LU, England

5   4   3   2

Printed in the United States of America

Negative numbers for illustrations obtained from the State Historical
Society of Wisconsin Iconographic Collections are as follows: illustration
1, WHi(x3)12922; illustration 3, WHi(x3)11494; illustration 4,
WHi(x3)10556; illustration 5, WHi(x3)12905; illustration 6, WHi(x3)12902;
illustration 8, WHi(x3)49381; illustration 9, WHi(x3)49330; illustration 10,
WHi(x3)12906; illustration 12 and cover, WHi(x3)49329.

Library of Congress Cataloging-in-Publication Data
Newton, James King, d. 1892.
    [Correspondence. Selections]
    A Wisconsin boy in Dixie: Civil War letters of James K. Newton /
edited by Stephen E. Ambrose.
        214 p.   cm.
    ''A North Coast book.''
    Includes bibliographical references and index.
    ISBN 0-299-02484-9
    1. Newton, James King, d. 1892—Correspondence. 2. Soldiers—
Wisconsin—Correspondence. 3. United States—History—Civil War,
1861-1865—Personal narratives. 4. Wisconsin—History—Civil War,
1861-1865—Personal narratives. 5. United States. Army. Wisconsin
Infantry Regiment, 14th (1862-1865) 6. United States—History—
Civil War, 1861-1865—Regimental histories. 7. Wisconsin—History—
Civil War, 1861-1865—Regimental histories. I. Title.
E601.N56   1995
973.7'81—dc20   94-24104

James K. Newton's letters, which are in the Abel Newton Papers in the State Historical Society Library, Madison, Wisconsin, were usually written in ink on paper of good quality. Newton's handwriting, perhaps because he had been a schoolteacher, is easily legible. It was Newton's custom to fill the pages of his letters as copiously as possible; as an aid to smooth reading, the letters reproduced here have been broken into paragraphs, and some punctuation has been added. In a few instances, words missing because of the mutilation of pages or the writer's oversight have been supplied in brackets. Miswritings obviously accidental, such as "thing" for "think," have been silently corrected.

Not all of the letters which Newton wrote during the war appear in these pages, and from those printed here some deletions have been made. Personal or family matters of little interest to the general reader have been omitted. To avoid repetition, many of Newton's references to his health—a subject of considerable importance during the Civil War, when sickness and disease claimed more lives than did bullets—have been eliminated, as have a number of his comments on the weather and his complaints about the lack of mail. To keep the focus on Newton himself, incidents which he mentioned but in which he was not personally involved have for the most part not been included. Two letters from Newton's brother Samuel, describing campaigns in which he participated, have been included. All deletions within the letters have been indicated.

The editor wishes to thank Dr. William B. Hesseltine of the University of Wisconsin, Dr. O. Lawrence Burnette, Jr., Miss Josephine Harper, and Miss Margaret Gleason of the staff of the State Historical Society of Wisconsin, Mrs. Elizabeth Groh of the Louisiana State University in New Orleans, and Mr. Donald M. Love, Secretary of Oberlin College, for their kind assistance. He is grateful to Mr. John Hunter of Madison for permission to reproduce the drawings of Alex Simplot, formerly in Mr. Hunter's private collection and now in the Wisconsin State Historical Society Museum, to Thomas Yoseloff, Inc., for permission to use the photograph of Logan's Mine from *The Photographic History of the Civil War,* and to the Cartographic Laboratory of the University of Wisconsin for preparing the maps.

S. E. A.

New Orleans, Louisiana
March, 1961

TABLE OF CONTENTS

INTRODUCTION

The Civil War is the central theme of American history; it was also the central theme in the lives of the boys who fought it. Nothing they had done before could compare with it, and nothing that happened to them afterwards could dim the memory of those glorious, tragic days. James K. Newton went off to war at eighteen, and spent four years in the Union army. What this meant to his development he partially realized; when the war was finally over, he reflected: "What an experience the last few years have been! I would not take any amount of money & have the events which have transpired in that length of time blotted out from my memory." Newton wrote of the war with verve, feeling, imagination, and insight. His letters to his parents conveyed to them—as they do to the modern reader —an intimate view of the excitement, the horror, the tragedy, the humor, and the importance of the American Civil War.

Newton was born and raised on a substantial farm in De

Pere, Wisconsin, where he enjoyed a happy family life. His father, Abel Newton, had come to Wisconsin as a missionary. Although both James's parents had been born in Massachusetts, all the children were born in Wisconsin. The family included three boys, Edward, older than James, and Samuel, younger; and five girls, Mercena and Mattie, both married at the time of the war, Minnie, who was teaching school, and Sarah and Marion, the "little girls." When the news of the bombardment of Fort Sumter reached De Pere, James was seventeen years old; he stood six feet tall, weighed over 180 pounds, and had light brown hair and hazel eyes. He made his living as a teacher in a one-room schoolhouse in Brown County.[1]

The boys of 1861 volunteered for diverse reasons; patriotism, social and family pressure, desire to escape the monotony of life on the frontier, financial gain—all played a part in inducing enlistment. Newton joined the army because of a combination of these and other motives. In 1861 he was mildly patriotic, but hardly fanatical. The citizens of De Pere expected all their young men to enlist. Newton's older brother had preceded him into the service, and by the fall of 1861 the young schoolteacher was determined to join up as soon as possible. On October 1, 1861, he enlisted in Company F of the Fourteenth Wisconsin Volunteer Infantry. As he had probably expected, he found the army different from, and more exciting than, life on the frontier.

---

[1] The information in this Introduction is taken from James K. Newton's Papers in the Wisconsin State Historical Society; 8th United States Census (1860), Brown County, Wisconsin, p. 456; letter of Donald M. Love, Secretary of Oberlin College, to the editor, November 7, 1958, in the possession of the editor; various pension claims made by Newton and his wife in the National Archives, Washington, D.C.; and *Roster of Wisconsin Volunteers, War of the Rebellion, 1861–1865* (2 vols., Madison, 1886), I, 787.

Newton and his company started off from De Pere with a
salute of three cheers for their home town, and even having
to spend their first night in the army crowded all together
in the tiny cabin of a boat to sleep (Newton called it "one
of the greatest times I ever went through") did not dampen
their enthusiasm. Newton reported that the company to
which he belonged was the "best drilled, best behaved, and
best looking" in the camp.

When he enlisted, and throughout the war, Newton retained a sense of proportion and balance. He never became
an abolitionist, nor did he allow social pressure to deter-
mine his attitudes. Neither did he become so enamoured
of army life that he did not hope for an end to the war.
"If the settlement of this war was left to the Enlisted men
of both sides," he remarked in 1863, "we would soon go
home."

In the midst of a war that rushed the United States into
the modern world, when pressure from every side forced
men to become a part of the conforming mass, Newton
remained an individual. A Lincoln supporter, he scorned
but did not hate Copperheads. He wished to see the South
defeated but not devastated. "I can't pity the rebels themselves," he said at Vicksburg, "but it does seem too bad for
the women and children in the city." Newton evaluated
for himself the experiences he was undergoing; his letters
are significant because he was never content to repeat the
common shibboleths of the day.

The young soldier spent the winter of 1861–62 training
in various Wisconsin camps. He enjoyed the new surround-
ings and delighted in describing them to the homefolks. In
March, 1862, he went to St. Louis and from there to Pittsburg Landing, Tennessee, where he fought in his first
battle, Shiloh. "All I need say about the 14th is that they

didn't run," Newton commented. After the engagement, he went on garrison duty at Corinth, Mississippi, recently evacuated by the Confederates, until the enemy attacked in October. Fighting with skirmishers, he was soon captured and shipped to Vicksburg. He was paroled and sent back to St. Louis. Under the terms of his parole he was able to go home to Wisconsin for a short visit.

In December, Newton was exchanged for a captured Confederate soldier, and returned to his regiment. He was soon taking part in General Ulysses S. Grant's campaign to capture Vicksburg, the last Confederate stronghold on the Mississippi River. Newton joined in various attempts to reach the city from the western bank of the river, all of which failed. In the spring he marched south of Vicksburg, crossed the river, and fought with the army to the gates of the city, where Grant set up a siege. Newton carefully recorded his experiences throughout the entire campaign, and dwelt upon one unsuccessful attempt to storm the Confederate works.

The "Devoted City," a sobriquet Vicksburg earned from Grant's soldiers, capitulated after enduring more than a month of siege. Newton spent the remainder of 1863 on garrison duty in Mississippi, and on December 11, 1863, after being promised a short furlough, re-enlisted. When he returned from a visit to De Pere, Newton joined General Nathaniel P. Banks's army in its unsuccessful attempt to destroy the Confederate armies in Louisiana and establish an army of occupation in Texas. The series of small, fruitless engagements disgusted him. "The famous 'Red River Expedition' is over at last & we are out of Banks' Dep't," he told his parents. "I hope we may never go near it again."

Newton spent the summer and fall of 1864 with General Frederick Steele, campaigning in Arkansas and Missouri against Confederate General Sterling Price. The elusive Confederate refused to join a pitched battle and the regiment spent most of its time marching. Newton found that he had become acclimated; in October the Wisconsin boy wrote from southern Missouri: "I hope that when I write again it will be from some other place a little further south; for I didn't enlist to soldier so far north as this."

From Missouri, Newton went to Tennessee in time for the Battle of Nashville and the pursuit of the routed Confederate army. In February, 1865, he returned to Vicksburg, then moved on to New Orleans, and finally to his last campaign, the siege of Mobile.

In July, 1865, Newton was commissioned a lieutenant; he spent the summer and fall of that year in Alabama as special commissioner for administering the amnesty oath. He was mustered out on October 9, 1865, and immediately entered Ripon Academy in Wisconsin. The next year he transferred to Oberlin College, Oberlin, Ohio, where he studied for five years. In 1873 he became a member of the Oberlin faculty as instructor in German and French—he became a professor in 1875—and remained there until 1888. One of Newton's Japanese students at Oberlin was so grateful to him for help received during his college years that in May, 1918, he established the James K. Newton Japanese Prize in his memory.

On August 10, 1870, Newton married a widow, Mrs. Frances Woodrow, who had graduated from Oberlin in 1859. In 1888, Newton retired and took his wife to California. He died on June 26, 1892, in Nordhoff, California, and is buried in Ojai, California.

The Civil War was the great experience of Newton's life, and during the course of it his character grew and developed. Between 1861 and 1866 he matured. His first war letters are brash, excitable, and not particularly perceptive; gradually he became an intelligent, capable, and informative writer. But he was never pretentious and was always careful in pronouncing judgment; when he did give an opinion it was worth while. He correctly saw that the struggle for Vicksburg was the military turning point of the war. On April 30, 1863, he commented that if matters turned out at Vicksburg "as we all hope they will the war will soon come to an end. And then 'hurrah for home.' " He was tremendously proud of the role he and his regiment played in capturing the city: "Our Reg't had the honor of leading the Brigade into the city. We all felt proud of it, I can tell you, for we had worked, and fought hard to obtain that privalege. . . ."

As the war progressed Newton developed a sense of responsibility towards his parents, who were having financial difficulties. Newton sent money home whenever he could, and his first thought when he became a sergeant was of the increase in pay. In 1863 he considered taking a commission in a Negro regiment because, as he told his parents, with the increase in pay "I could help you along a great deal more than I am now able to do. . . ." However, his mother "took a decided stand" against his joining a "Black Regiment." Newton wanted to stay with his own regiment, and did not press the matter.

Despite the temptations of the "vices of the camp" Newton retained his religious convictions. While participating in the siege of Vicksburg he confessed to his mother: "I have long been under deep concern for my sins, but I have learned to put my trust in God believing that He will blot them out of the 'book of His remembrance' if sincerely repented of. I hope and trust that God will forgive all my sins for the sake of Jesus Christ our Redeemer. . . ."

He also kept his sense of humor, and made unpleasant

situations bearable by concentrating on their ridiculous aspects. His account of the Battle of Corinth is not only accurate and significant, but amusing as well. And in the fall of 1864, when Newton and his good friend John Ryan both suffered from a lack of food and from the ague, instead of complaining, Newton reported: "When Ryan has a better appetite than usual, I have to remind him of the fact, by 'hoping that he'll have the ague soon.' By the way, my appetite is pretty good now, I guess, for he has wished several times lately 'that he could catch me shaking.' You see we have the ague by turns. When Ryan's sick I eat all the rations, & when I'm sick, Ryan eats them. But sometimes, you see, we feel pretty well at the same times & then the rations cant hold out any how we can fix it. . . ."

Newton's patriotism and understanding of the issues involved grew slowly but steadily during the war. In his first year in the army he gave no indication of any political awareness; by the fall of 1862, after he had helped throw a slaveholder out of camp, he could remark: "To tell the truth we are just getting into the spirit of the war. . . ." In 1864 he voted Republican, partly because the Republicans were the party of the Union, partly because he had come to scorn the Copperheads, or northern peace Democrats, because they slighted the work of the army and the magnititude of the victories it was winning. After giving the first vote of his life to Abraham Lincoln, Newton told his parents: "In doing so I felt that I was doing my country as much service as I have ever done on the field of battle." He thought the army could complete its work soon if the Copperheads suffered a "whipping so that they would stay whipped . . ." and believed that a Republican victory would show that "we [the army], constituting as we do the war power of the Union, will be upheld by the masses of the people. . . ." But if the Democrats won, Newton was certain that the army would go all out to finish its job before March 4, 1865. And when the war was over, Newton firmly expressed his hatred for the Confederate leaders—he hoped the government would hang Jefferson Davis. For Lincoln, Newton developed deep feelings of love and respect. After hearing of Lincoln's assassination, he said: "At the north I doubt not his death is felt to be a great national calamity, but nowhere is such sincere sorrow felt as here in the army. No man, not even Grant himself, possesses the entire love of the army as did President Lincoln." And in a final sentence, Newton revealed just how much he had grown in maturity, in intelligence, in understanding. Of the martyred Lincoln he wrote: "We mourn him not only as a President but as a man, for we had learned to love him as one possessed of every manly principle." By 1865 James K. Newton was a tough, hardened, efficient soldier; he was also a sensitive individual.

A WISCONSIN BOY IN DIXIE

CIVIL WAR LETTERS OF JAMES K. NEWTON

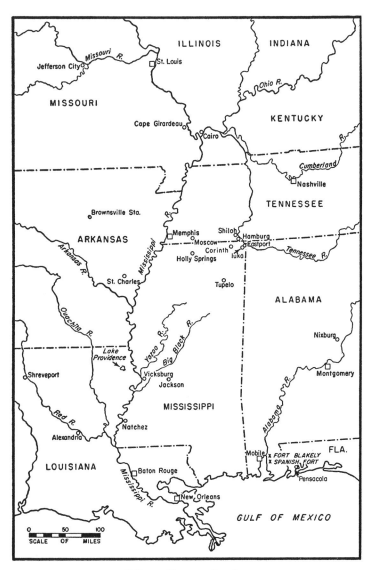

Where Newton fought

CHAPTER ONE

OFF TO WAR

Camp Hamilton, Nov 17 1861

Dear Father & Mother
& all of the rest of the family,

   . . . We started from Depere about three o'clock on
thursday afternoon. All of the men seemed to be in good
spirits and all united in giving Depere three cheers at
starting. The boat "Fanny Fisk" was pretty well crowded
but we got along very well untill night when we had one
of the greatest times that I ever went through. As soon as
night came on the men began to pile into the Cabin to find
a place to sleep. The first lot went under the table and lay
as thick as they could edgeways. Then a lot of them got
onto the tables and lay there. Then there was a little room
off from the Cabin and they filled that full and the rest lay
around the floor wherever they could get a chance. For my

self I got a place under the table. I lay there as long as I thought there was no danger of smothering. When I thought there was I got up and went out and walked the deck until morning. . . .

We arrived in Fondulac about five o'clock on friday morning. In about half an hour it began to snow and it snowed all the while that we were marching up to the camp. After we got here the sun came out and it was warm and pleasant all of the rest of the day. About 9 o'clock we had breakfast and all the rest of the day we were putting up tents.

Every tent, (with the exception of the officers tents) is round and is about 18 feet in diameter at the bottom and tapers up to a point at hight of about 15 feet. There is a sheet iron stove for each tent with two lengths of stove pipe for each stove which is hardly enough as it does not reach high enough to carry all of the smoke out but after we get charcoal I think it will go a great deal better. We have good beef and potatoes, bread and butter to eat and coffee to drink and all that we want of it too.

There are 18 men in the tent that I stay in. We are under Corporal Robert Beattie. We have 2 tin pails 1 camp kettle 2 wash bowls (and a towel for each man) in each tent besides a knife and fork, tin cup and tin plate for each man. Besides this we have 2 axes 2 shovels 2 spades and 2 hatchets for the use of each company. . . .

After being here two days Col Wood remarked to Capt Lawton [1] that he (Lawton) had the best drilled, best behaved, and best looking company not only in this Reg but also in the third Reg which was quartered here last June. . . .

---

[1] Colonel David E. Wood was from Fond du Lac; Captain Joseph G. Lawton, from De Pere.

I must close as it is dinner time so good bye for the present.

Your Affectionate Son,

James K. Newton

Camp Wood, Fond du Lac, Nov 29th 1861

Dear Father and Mother,

. . . Capt. Lawton has been to Madison for the last four days. He got back last night. He says that the mustering officer will be here next week when we will be mustered into the U.S. service. He says that we will be paid immediately afterward. We have not got any clothes yet except some shoes and socks and a shirt apiece but we expect to get them all next week.

I spent a great thanksgiving day yesterday I guess I never spent such an one before. I had to drill all of the forenoon and untill four o'clock in the afternoon. Then I got a pass and went down town in the evening and had a piece of mince pie which is the only piece that I have had since I left Depere but then I get all that I want of meat & beans & bread & rice &c so that there is no danger of my starving at present. . . .

I hope that you will answer this as soon as you get it. The name of our camp has been changed to Camp Wood.

I must close now so good bye for the present Your affectionate Son

James

The regiment remained in Fond du Lac and James went home for Christmas.

Headquarters Camp Wood
14th Reg't Wis Vols
Fond du Lac Jan 5th 1861 [1862]

Dear Father and Mother

This is the first chance that I have had to write to you since I left home or I should have written sooner. We have been put right through ever since we got here to make up for the time that we were away I suppose. I was put on guard the day after I got here; that was New Years day you know. . . .

The guns were distributed to the regt day before yesterday and it has taken all of my spare time since then to clean mine up and get it ready for use. They are called the Belgian rifled musket and we have to go through the light infantry drill the same as though they were rifles. When we got them they were covered with tallow both inside and out. We have got all of our accoutrements now but the knapsacks and we will get them tomorrow. . . .

One of our Corporals run the guard the other day and he has been put back in the ranks for doing it. His name is S. C. Hayward of Oconto. There is a great deal of talk about it in camp today and he was put on guard today as a private. I have written this letter in a hurry so you must excuse bad writing. I shall ever remain your affectionate son

James K. Newton

Headquarters Camp Wood
14th Regt Wis Vols
Fond du Lac Jany 18th, 1862

Dear Father & Mother

I rec'd your letter yesterday and I now take the first opportunity of answering it. I began to think that you were
never going to answer my letter.

I hope that you are all as well at home as I am up here.
It has been pretty cold up here for the last week. The
thermometer stood at 28° below o last Tuesday, that was
the coldest weather we have had since we came up here and
I hope we won't have any colder weather this winter. If we
do I guess we will have to make different arrangements
about our quarters. We have got another kind of stoves
since the cold weather came on, we threw the old ones out
doors and then made them get us some more. Before night
we had another kind altogether so that we manage to keep
warm now without any trouble. . . .

One of our men ran away last Monday. . . .

The Col says that we will get our pay next week but we
have been put off so long that I dont believe much that
they tell us now. Although I guess it is about time that we
got it. They say that we will be paid off to the first of Jany.
If they do we will get considerable all at once. . . .

I have not time to write any more as the Tattoo is beat-
ing now and I will have to fall out for roll call before it
stops.

Love to all the family
Your affect Son

J. K. Newton

Camp Wood Fond du Lac Jan. 29th
1862

My Dear Parents

. . . I hope that you both are enjoying as good health as I am at present. I wish that I could say that all of the boys were enjoying as good health as I am but I cant, there are ten or a dozen of them down in the hospital and half a dozen others that will have to go down before long. Dr. Cameron [2] has just gone out from the tent, he came in to see Charley Beattie. He says that Charley has the measles, and he is getting ready to go down to the hospital. There are eight or ten others that have the mumps, and others that dont know what ails them, and there are some others that are only pretending sick so that they can get rid of duty, but I dont believe they will make much by it.

. . . I am much obliged to you for that night cap that you sent me . . . it is just the thing that I have been wanting ever since I came up here. . . . We have been getting ready for the mustering officer for the last three days. I have heard that he is here on the ground now. Whether it is true or not I dont know. . . .

Your affectionate Son

James K. N.

Camp Wood
Fond du Lac, Feby 24th 1862

Dear Father & Mother;

I rec'd your welcome letter this morning and I have embraced the first opportunity to answer it. I was on guard

---

[2] Dr. Duncan D. Cameron of La Crosse.

yesterday and last night, it is the first time that I have had to stand guard on sunday since we have been up here. It happened lucky though this time for if I had not been on guard I could not have answered your letter today. You see all of the boys that stand guard one day are excused from duty for half of the next day, and they can either have a pass to go down town or they can stay at home. I preferred the latter. I am enjoying as good health as I could wish to. I hope you are no worse off in that respect than I am.

If we stay here much longer we shall have to get a canoe to go around the streets in. Yesterday and the day before were warm days and the water stood ankle deep all over the camp, that is only a foretaste of what it will be in less than ten days.

Day before yesterday was Washingtons birth day, and the city of Fond du Lac gave a picnic for the soldiers, and such a picnic as it was! At one o'clock the Regt was called out and formed in hollow square and the Col read Washingtons Farewell Address. We were then formed in line of battle again and Co A. was feasted on pies and cakes and cheese and cold ham and such like right before the rest of the Regt and after they got through the leavings were passed around to the rest. (You know Co A is the co that was got up in Fond du Lac.) There was not half as much for the whole Regt as there was carried away from the factory the morning after the party that we had in Depere. Every Co in the Regt took it as an insult, more so probably than they would have done if the people of F. du Lac had not done all they could to run down the Regt. Some of the Companies gave three groans for F. du Lac before they dispersed.

Afternoon. I have just come in from inspection. The Col has been getting us ready for inspection by the Governor. The report is that both he and the paymaster are to be here tonight and the Regt are to escort him up to the camp. If they get here tonight it is very likely that we will be paid off this week and I dont think that we will stay here many days after that so you must not be surprised if I dont come down home again. . . . I have come to the end of my paper so I must bid you good bye. Your Affectionate Son

James

March 11th/62
Headquarters Camp Benton
St Louis, Mo.

Dear Father & Mother

I started from Camp W. with the rest of the Regt on Saturday morning. We were called up at one o'clock in the morning to get ready for marching. We struck the tents and sent them off and had every thing done long before daylight. As soon as it was light enough to see well we were marched down to the depot and loaded onto the cars. The day before, the people of Fond du Lac had got together and done up bread and butter & meat & cheese & cake and *other things to numerous to mention* into bundles and after we were all on board they passed through the cars and gave each man a bundle. That had to do us for breakfast and dinner and then we got supper at Chicago on the cars after marching through the city for two hours—it made some of the boys grumble a little but that didn't do them any good.

I like the looks of Chicago, there is so many pretty buildings in it. One of the buildings that I noticed was the Republican Wigwam where Old Abe was nominated. I like the way St. Louis is laid out a great deal better than Chicago but it has not near as fine looking buildings. You may look what way you will and wont see anything but red brick.

We started from Chicago at 9 o'clock in the evening and traveled all night and the next day until 5 o'clock when we reached Alton (Illinois). We then went on board a steamboat and we laid there at the dock until 3 o'clock in the morning when the boat got under way and we went down the river to St. Louis where we arrived about sunrise. At ten o'clock we were taken off the boat and had to march 3½ miles to camp. Some of the boys gave out before we got here and had to be brought out here by one of the street cars.

March 12th/62   Dear Parents,

I was obliged to break off yesterday because I had to go on extra duty and I have taken the first chance to finish it. The boys here in camp dont seem to realize that they are in the enemy's country. The first day that we came the camp was full of pedlars selling pies and cakes, apples and oranges and all such stuff, and because it was cheap the boys began to stuff it down and the consequence was that a good many of them were taken with the cholera morbus and then there was a great [cry] that they were poisined. The [doctor] told them that it was very likely that they might expect all such things now. He said that in order to keep them from eating everything that comes along and not because there was any danger of there being poisined.

The weather here is as warm as it is in June up where you are. I am sure I dont want any hotter weather than it has been since we came here. It is quite a change to leave two ft. of snow behind you and then within two days to go where it is as warm as it is in summer where you are.

In my opinion such a sudden change is going to make a good many sick before we get used to it. . . . There was three men died last night in a private house close by the camp, they belonged to one of the Illinois Regts that are encamped here. Some of the men say that they were poisined but whether it is so or not I dont know. I guess there is a good deal of imagination about it.

I almost forgot to tell you the name of our camp. The real name is Benton Barracks but as we are in our tents and not in barracks we call it Camp Benton, so you see the camp and the Barracks are separate from each other. The barracks were built last spring by General Fremont [3] and are calculated to hold 35000 men. There is between 12 & 15 thousand here now but for all that they wouldn't let us go into them so we had to pitch our tents, and now we are as comfortable as if we were in the barracks. . . .

We dont expect to stay here more than three days longer at most though for all we know about it we may stay here 3 weeks.

It is almost drill time and I shall have to close. . . .
Your Affectionate Son

James K. Newton

---

[3] Major-General John C. Fremont, the first commander of the Western Department.

CHAPTER TWO

SHILOH

Pittsburgh Landing
Somewhere in the wilderness
in west Tennessee
Saturday, April 12, 1862

Dear Father & Mother
& all the Family

It is with a feeling of thankfulness that I sit down to write these few lines; to think that I have been spared when so many others have fallen. I suppose by the time you receive this that you will have heard all about the battle of Pittsburgh Landing (as I suppose it will be called).[1] All that I need say about the 14th is that they *didn't run.*

---

[1] Although the battle took place at Pittsburg Landing, it took its name from a small church standing on the Union right—Shiloh. The battle was won by the Union on the second day of fighting. For a

Last Sunday morning about daylight the cannon began to boom up the river about ten miles & every one began to speculate as to what was the matter up there. In a few hours all sorts of rumors reached the camp but from what source I dont know. One report was that the 18th Wis was all cut to pieces & that report was as near true as it could be. The next report was that our men were completely whipped out & that they were running in every direction & after we got up here we found it just about so. About 4 o'cl'k in the afternoon there came an order for us to get ready to march in half an hour to reinforce our men up the river. We dropped every thing at once and started for the boat taking nothing with us but our arms & blankets. After we got down to the boat we found that we would have to wait for more men to come because they wouldn't let one Regt go up the river alone, so we waited until about 9 o'cl'k in the evening when they got together 17,000 men & we came up the river in company. While we lay at the dock in Savanna a boat came down the river with the Col & Lieut Col of the 18th Wis, both of them badly wounded. The Col has since died.

When we reached Pittsburgh, which we did about 11 o'cl'k that night, we found that our force still held the bank of the river where they were formed in line of battle, while the Secesh had formed another line of battle about 100 rods in front of us. Our Regt was formed on the right of the line where we stood all night while it rained like shot all the time, we didn't think until then what good service our India rubber blankets would do us. As it was we kept

description of the battle, see Robert Underwood Johnson and Clarence Clough Buel, eds., *Battles and Leaders of the Civil War* (4 vols.; new edition; New York, 1956), I, 465–611, especially the article by General Ulysses S. Grant.

ourselves comparatively dry though we had to stand up all the time to do so.

Well daylight came at last but it was an awful long time coming. As soon as our pickets could see the Secesh pickets they began to fire into them. They returned the fire for a while but finally retired. Our pickets then fell back upon the main body. In a few minutes our whole line began to move toward the enemy. Our Regt was held back as a reserve for a while, & there we lay right in the mud while a perfect storm of shot and shell grape & canister flew by in the air over our heads.

A battery of artillery soon came to our assistance & opened on the Rebels, they kept it up nearly half an hour before our battery silenced theirs, when all at once a lot of Secesh who had advanced under cover of their battery opened fire right in our faces.

The order was then given for us to advance & then we found out what it was to fight a battle. The first man that was wounded in our company was Chas Vincent; he was shot through the leg. All that I remember for a while after that was that I loaded as fast as possible and wherever I saw a Secesh I shot at him, & that was what every one there did. ·

There is no use in trying to describe the battle because I can not do it. All I know about it is that we drove the rebels & they drove us & then we would drive them again. We charged on one of their batteries and took it & then they charged in their turn and we couldn't hold it so we spiked the guns & set fire to their cartridges so that they couldn't use it on us any more. The next time we charged on that battery we were supported & kept it. We were advanceing & retreating all the time until afternoon, before we got the upper hand of the Secesh but when we once got it we drove them rapidly until 4 o'cl'k in [the] afternoon when our Cavalry & artillery came in ahead of us and pursued them until after dark while we fell back to the river and got together as well as possible.

It rained that night and the next night & we stood out in line both nights & then the worst of it was that we couldn't get any thing to eat but hard bread and not much of that.

The morning after the fight the Regt was got together and it was found that we had lost between 20 & 30 killed and somewhere about 100 wounded. One Co lost 5 killed. Our Co lost two killed & five wounded. . . .

As for myself I came off with out a scratch and I am sure I dont know why it was for I stood as good a chance as any of them to get hurt. A good many of the boys came to the conclusion *after the battle* that the Secesh shot awful careless with their guns, and I guess all of the Co are perfectly satisfied as to what war is & they would be willing to have the war brought to an end so they could be discharged and sent home.

Dennis Murphy distinguished himself considerably on the field, in fact he behaved nobly. He was the one who avenged poor Putnam. Dennis shot down the rebel who murdered Putnam before he could take his gun from his face. I hear that his name was sent in the report to Washington for brave conduct on the field.

Our Capt behaved as brave as any of them. There was a good deal of speculation as to how he would behave on the field of battle. A good many folks thought that he wouldn't "stand fire" but he did a good deal better than others that were thought to be so brave but when they came to be tried it was found they were not made of the right stuff. . . .

Uncle's advice to us boys was to put our trust in the Lord and "give them Jesse." I guess by the time that you receive this he will have found out that we *followed* his

advice before he gave it. If you get hold of a paper with
the perticulars of the battle in it I wish you would send it
down here. All we know about the battle is what we saw &
that wasn't much, so I would like to see a paper if possible
to see what we did do.

I suppose you are making sugar "like everything" nowadays. How I would like to call in and see you about this
time and get some to eat. I got a piece of soft bread yesterday for the first time since I left St. Louis. I needn't tell
you, I guess, *that I could eat it without butter.* . . .

Give my respects to all enquiring friends. With much
love,

I remain

Your Affectionate Son

James

Pittsburgh Landing
Saturday, May 3d/62

Dear Father & Mother,

   . . . I was in St. Louis last week. I went down with a
squad of twenty men under Lieut Harrison. We went
down as a guard over forty six prisoners. We delivered
them over safe into the hands of the Provost Guard of the
city and then we were allowed to run around for a day before we had to go back.

The first thing that I done was to set out for Benton
Barracks. I found Ed [2] & all the rest of the boys looking as
fat and hearty as ever though Ed had one of his bad colds.
He said it was the fourth one he had had while he had been

---

[2] His brother Edward, member of the First Wisconsin Cavalry.

in St. Louis. . . . The boys all came to the conclusion that I didn't look near as fat as I did when I left St. Louis a few weeks before. I could only stay with Ed one day & then I had to leave for Tenn.

We had a first rate time coming back for we didn't have to do a thing all of the way up but eat and sleep and you had better believe that we laid into it well. I slept more in those 4 days & nights then I had done for two weeks before & I believe it did me good too for I have felt a great deal better ever since.

I suppose you have made "lots" of maple sugar by this time. I hope that I shall be on hand to help you make it by the time another spring comes around. That is if we get "Uncle Sams thrashing" done by that time & I guess we will if we only keep on at the rate that we are going now. I should think that the rebels must be awfully discouraged by this time, but some of the prisoners that we take dont seem to show it much. . . .

It is almost time for roll call and I must close, give my love to Saml, Sarah & Marion [3] & keep a good share for yourself.

Your affectionate Son,

James K. Newton

Pittsburg Landing May 6th/62

Dear Father & Mother

. . . I suppose by the time this reaches you *"Mr"* Bowers will have reached home as well as *"Mr"* Lawton.[4] I guess

---

[3] His younger brother and sisters at home.

[4] George W. Bowers of De Pere and Captain Lawton both resigned immediately after Shiloh. Newton seemed to have been impressed

the people of Depere must have felt mighty cheap, after making such a fuss over Lawtons arrival, to find out that he had been forced to resign, instead of doing so of his own accord. I have heard a good many men in our Co threaten to smash those gold spectacles for him if they ever get home again. He went off owing about one third of the men in the Co. besides swindling us out of the Co funds. There was over 100 dollars of company funds that he did not render any account of to Capt Camm [5] at all. When he left he gave Capt Camm an order on the Sutler for $30.00. He said that was all of the funds that were left. It seems that he had given the Sutler a draft on his brother Gus. Lawton & when the Sutler presented the draft for payment Gus. Lawton refused to pay. The reason he gave was that "Joe Lawton never paid his debts." So of course the Sutler would not pay either. That was a nice dodge wasn't it.

A good many of the men who knew what kind of a man he was thought that *"he would not be so mean as to cheat the men in his own Co,"* & so they trusted him more than they would otherwise have done. Well he didn't get only $1.44 out of me so I cant growl much. Some of the men he owed as much as 12 & 15 dollars.

Bowers wasn't near so bad but the only reason was that he didn't know how so well. I guess he had not had so much practice as Lawton had, but it was hard telling which was the biggest Coward.

That story about Lawtons being so brave was all a hoax, as soon as the battle commenced he was seen making for the river about as fast as his legs would carry him. When

by Lawton's conduct on the field of battle, and his "swindling us out of the Co funds" may have affected his later judgment.

[5] Newton probably means James Camm of Company F, who was commissioned as lieutenant on April 18, 1862.

asked where he was going he replied "that he was going down to the river to *draw rations,* so that the boys could have something to eat as soon as they were done fighting." Very thoughtful, wasn't he.

As for Bowers he was taken with the fever and ague that morning. I should think he *might have chosen almost any other kind of disease rather than that. That seems to me to be rather too significant.*

Well if I am going to write often I cant afford to write very long letters so I am going to stop pretty soon. My health is very good at present for all we have to do so much guard duty nowadays. The boys are all well, as usual.

"I'll bet" we have pleasanter weather here than you do in Wis. just now. The Sun shines as bright as can be & the trees are all leaved out. Besides that the apples & peaches are as big as the end of my thumb. Love to all.

Your affectionate Son James

Pittsburg May 14th/62

My Dear Parents;

. . . Our Reg't was paid off last Sunday. I sent twenty dollars off by express along with ten other men to be delivered to Mr Cooley.[6] You can get it without any trouble, I suppose, by calling on him for it. There was $180.00 sent to him by the 11 men. We were afraid to send it by letter for fear that you would not get it. It cost us just 18 cts apiece to send it. I thought I had better keep the rest as I have to spend money once in a while.

. . . Our Reg't is almost "gin out," I dont believe we

---

[6] Possibly the father of Oscar Cooley of Company F.

could muster 300 effective men if we should try. The Col
has gone home sick with the bloody flux. There are several
other men in the Regt sick with the same disease. It is very
prevalent down here.

I guess you would like to know something about what is
going on out to Corinth. Well they have been fighting out
there off and on for nearly a week now. Most of it is
skirmishing, at least they call it so, but I call it all fighting,
especially when I hear the big guns roaring.

I heard to day that our troops intend to walk into
Corinth either tomorrow or the day after. They seem to
think that the Secesh have kept them out about long
enough. You may expect to hear of a big battle out there in
a few days.[7] You need not feel alarmed about me in the
least as our reg't could not leave this post if we wanted to
so there is no danger of our being in the fight. I can tell you
there is not many who want to take part in it either. The
men were all satisfied the last time we went into battle
without trying it over again. . . .

Give my love to all the family and remember me as your

affectionate Son James

Pittsburg May 26th/62

My Dear Parents

I have just finished reading your very welcome letter &
I have set myself right down to answer it. . . .

---

[7] The "big battle" at Corinth never came off. General Henry W.
Halleck besieged the city from three sides, and was in constant fear
of an attack by the Confederates, whom he outnumbered almost two
to one.

Our Regt is falling away pretty fast, they send off between 40 & 50 every ten days. There is about 300 of us left to do duty & one quarter of those are not able to do the duty that we have to do. We bury from one to three almost every day. We have not lost any that I know of from our Co unless some of those that we sent off have died since. When you remember that a little over two months ago we numbered 980 good sound men & now we do not number over three hundred men that are able to do duty, it seems that we have been going down hill pretty fast. It is a common report in camp that we are going to be sent north to recruit but how soon we will be sent up there I dont know. . . .

I suppose a few of those reports as to how our officers conducted themselves on the battlefield must be true, but as I dont know what the reports are I shall go on and tell what I know to be the truth because I saw it with my own eyes.

The Capt marched us up off from the boat & set on a box of cartridges all sunday night in the rain. In the morning he was a bright as could be for he had a chance to sleep & I dont know of one of the other men that slept at all that night. The next morning he led us out on the battlefield all right enough. When the order was given for us to charge, we started on, firing as we went. The first order that I heard given by the Capt was to "cease firing." I turned round and there he stood with his revolver cocked in his right hand & there he stood swinging his pistol & calling on the men to "cease firing." Just then the Lt. Col came riding along & when he saw our hesitation he cried out "Give it to them, boys," with that we started & we did not stop for the Capt or any one else.

The Capt said afterward that he "thought they were our own men." I dont remember of seeing him again that day, but one of the boys told me afterward that he met the Capt running for the river, & he asked him where he was going, the Capt said "I am going down to the River to draw rations so that the boys can have something to eat as soon as they have done fighting." There is one thing about it, we did not see any rations until after dark that night, nor did we see the Capt either for that matter.

I heard from very good authority that the Capt went to the Col in the midst of the battle and told him that "he did not think he was doing justice to his family by staying where he was in danger of his life from one of his own men." The man that he meant was Sergt Avery. What he has against Avery I dont know but he has acted with a very revengefull spirit toward him. Avery would have been 2nd Lieut if it had not been for what Capt Lawton said about him. . . .

As for Bowers there is no doubt but what he is an arrant Coward. He had been complaining of being sick for 3 or 4 days before the battle but he was so that he could be around all the time & his cheeks looked as red as ever. I dont believe he was near as sick as I was that day but he couldn't be got to go on the battlefield though he did not go down to Savannah as the paper says but about noon on monday there was a lot of stragglers from different Regts got together and formed in a kind of Co & as Bowers was the only officer they could see walking around *doing nothing* they called on him to lead on to the battle but *he was so sick just about that time that he couldn't walk* so they didn't go just because they could not find an officer to lead them.

Lieut Harrison was on the battlefield all day. The paper does not praise him any too much, only a person might say that he was in command of the Co all day instead of in the afternoon as the paper said. . . .

Give my love to all the family & remember me as Your ever Loving Son

James

Pittsburg June 2nd/62

Dear Parents;

It has not been many days since I wrote you quite a long letter, but I suppose you wont scold much if I dont wait for an answer to my last letter as I have come to the conclusion that it wont hurt me to write every chance I can get. I am sure I dont know what I should do if I did not get a letter once in a while. I am afraid I would get homesick and that is the worst kind of sickness a person could have down here. . . .

Our forces have taken quite a number of prisoners within a few days. We have over two hundred to guard now with a fair prospect of more tomorrow. Gen Pope's Division took five thousand prisoners day before yesterday. Last Friday our troops took possession of Corinth. They found it almost entirely deserted by the rebels, but it seems they had not been gone long for Gen Mitchell sent word to Gen Halleck that he had surrounded eight thousand of them but his force was not large enough to take them all, but that he could hold them in check until noon if he (Gen Halleck) would send on reinforcements. They were sent on immediately and must have reached him in time but we have not heard whether the rebels were all taken or not yet.[8]

---

[8] The great majority of the Confederates escaped Major-General Ormsby M. Mitchel's pursuit.

And, *again,* word came last night that quite a large portion of the rebels who left Corinth, amounting to somewhere near thirty thousand, had been surrounded in a swamp a few miles from Cor and could be starved out in a day or two; whether this last report is true or not I cant tell but I hope it is so.[9] If the rebel army is broken up like that we will soon have the whole of them but I can hardly believe it. They know better than to break all up like that it seems to me, but we are *bound to whip them* and I think they will give it up themselves pretty soon. If they dont they have better courage than I give them credit for.

It is late & I must close so good bye

I remain Your affectionate Son

J. K. Newton

Pittsburg June 18th:/62

My Dear Parents

I have been trying to get a chance to write to you for a long time but I could not get a chance or you may be sure I would have improved it. As it is I am *taking* time to write to you when I have *lots* of other things to do.

We dont have as much time to write now as we used to have. We have to go on guard every other day regular, and besides that it takes all of our extra time to keep ourselves clean. (When I say ourselves I include our arms and equip-

---

[9] General Halleck himself started the rumor, later claiming that he had received a telegram from Major-General John Pope, declaring the prisoners were already captured. Pope denied having sent it, and a continuing and never reconciled controversy between the two generals began.

ments, clothes and everything else that belongs to us). So you see it takes a person almost all day to get ready to go on guard the next day. No one is allowed to come out on guard or dress parade without having his boots blacked, his clothes well brushed, and his gun so bright *that you can see your face in it,* and it is no fool of a job to do it either. For all that I never enjoyed better health than I do at present. One thing I have found out, that the best way to keep in good health down here is to keep in good spirits. As sure as one of the men get a little homesick and down-hearted they are sure to be sick. . . .

I am so sorry to hear that Pa has been sick. I hope by the time this reaches you that he will be restored to health. I hope you got that 20 dollars that I sent you, it was all left to Mr Cooley's honesty. If we stay here three weeks longer we will be paid again and I will try and send you some more.

There is a great deal of talk about our going to Memphis though whether we will go there or not I dont know. I am sure I dont care where we go as long as we are helping Uncle Sam along. I have got so that I can be contented anywhere. . . .

With love to all the family, I remain,

Your affectionate Son J. K. Newton

CHAPTER THREE

RUNNING ALL OVER
SECESSIA

On July 24, 1862, the Fourteenth Wisconsin moved from Pittsburg Landing to Hamburg, Tennessee, a few miles south of the landing on the Tennessee River.

Hamburg August 13th/62

Dear Father & Mother

I rec'd your kind letter dated July 25th nearly one week ago and this is the first opportunity I have had of answering it.

I was in hopes that I could keep out of the cook house all the time as I had kept out so long, but I was called on last week to take my turn at cooking so I had to go & I have had all I could do ever since but I wont have to stay much longer for the Capt got three "niggers" yesterday to

27

cook for the Co. but they did not know anymore about cooking than a child would so I have had to stay in there with them to "boss the job." Since then I have went by the name of *"nigger driver."* If the niggers come into camp for a week as fast as they have been coming for two days past we will soon have a waiter for every man in the Regt.

One of those who are in our cook house says that he was sold 4 years ago by his own Father for $1,400. He is nearly as white as I am and he has none of the negro peculiarities about him either. Now if that aint nearly as hard a story as you read in books so often, I would like to know what is.

A few days ago there was two slaves came into camp and said that they had run away, and they wanted to go to work for someone so that they wouldn't have to go back. One of the officers took them and set them to work. The next day a man came into camp and wanted to know where those two niggers were who came into camp the day before. He was told that we didn't keep such men as him in camp and that we would give him just five minutes to leave camp. He did not leave in that time so we had the pleasure of booting him out of camp. He has not been seen around since. To tell the truth we are just getting into the spirit of the war.

By the [way] they are raising troops up north I should think they intended to push on the war as fast as possible.

It is almost suppertime and I will have to close. . . With love to all the family I remain

Your Loving Son

J. K. Newton

Hamburg August 19th 1862

My Dear Father & Mother

The mail has just arrived that brought your welcome letter & I have commenced to answer it right off. I never have come so near wishing I never had enlisted as I did after I got through reading your letter. I declare its too bad to even think of either of you doing any more work, & if I had my way about it I am sure you would not. I cant help thinking what a good-for-nothing piece of humanity I was that I did not go to work & do something while I was at home, but I was lazy then, & thought of nothing but how little I could do, instead of how much, as I had ought to. Anyhow it seems to me as though I could do twice as much now as I used to do & not hurt me in the least. And now it does not seem as though we were doing much good to the U.S. or anyone else either. Here we have been kept right in this place all the time while the other Reg'ts have been doing the work & getting all the honor of it too. You dont know how it wears on the boys. And now, what I am most afraid of is, that they will draft Samuel, and then you would be left entirely destitute of help. . . .

There was quite a sad accident happened in camp today. One of the new recruits who came from Wis (he got here three days ago) was cleaning his gun. It had a load in it and he was trying to draw the ball, when it went off & ramrod and all went through his right hand, tearing it all to peaces. The Dr's have concluded to cut off the hand and have done with it but if it was mine I am sure they could not, for I believe that a poor hand is better than none at all. . . .

With love to all the family I remain your Loving Son

J. K. Newton

Camp near Corinth Aug 31st/62

My Dear Parents;

I have been expecting a letter from you for some time, but as it does not come I guess I must write again. We have had quite a time down here since I wrote last. In the first place we have moved from Hamburg and now we are camped about one mile and a half from Corinth in a nice pleasant grove about forty rods from Maj Gen'l Grant's Headquarters.[1] It would be a first rate place to camp in only for one thing and that is the want of water. We have to go more than a mile and a half for water, and after we get it, it is not fit to drink.

We have been assigned to the second brigade of the sixth division. The second brigade is commanded by Col Oliver and the Division by Brig Gen'l McArthur.[2] Our Reg't and the 18th Wis are in the same Brigade. How many other Reg'ts there are in the Brigade I dont know.

There was quite an excitement raised about three days ago. There was a dispatch came to Headq'rs saying that the Rebels were tearing up the rail road track down near Bethel and our Regt rec'd orders to go down and put a stop to it. The long roll was beat and the Reg't all turned out, although we had been in camp here only one day and we were all tired out with the march from Hamburg. As [for] myself I could not go on account of having a big blood boil on my knee. The dispatch said that the Rebels were only about five miles from here, but instead of five, they marched fifteen miles that night and then to cap the climax

---

[1] Ulysses S. Grant, to whom Halleck—who in July went to Washington to take up his new duties as general-in-chief—had given command of troops in western Tennessee and northern Mississippi.

[2] John M. Oliver; John McArthur.

they did not meet with a single Rebel. I guess if they had they would have whipped them out in less than no time for they felt just like fighting about that time. They laid under the trees that night without anything to eat or drink and not half of the boys had their coats with them.

In the morning they started on again but they did not march far before they came to a plantation. The next order that the boys rec'd was to "break ranks and go to cooking." One of the boys was rather astonished and asked the Col what they were going to cook. "Why," said the Col, *"dont you see the pigs & sheep and chickens running around here."* The boys did not need another hint but straitway went to *cooking.* Some of them were pretty well tired out, so they laid down in the shade and *made the niggers cook for them.* There were about a doz bee hives at the same place so that the boys had all the honey they wanted. If it had been an Union man it would have been too bad to use up his property so, but as it was it was all right, for the owner was away from home with the Guirillas. The Reg't stayed at that place all day and came home on the cars at night.

Today is muster day and the Reg't have gone over to have Inspection and Review with the 18th. I could not walk over there so I have done the next best thing which is to write to you. My knee is getting better every day since the Dr lanced it so I hope to be able to do duty in a few days. . . .

I hope they wont draft Samuel if they go to drafting at all, that is the most that I am afraid of now. . . . I guess there must be considerable excitement in Depere about this time. What few papers we see are full of reports about the excitement that the war news creates in the northern cities. . . .

If I get a chance I will have a likeness taken & send it to

you so that you can see for yourself whether the climate agrees with me down here.

Your affectionate Son J. K. Newton

*Head Quarters 14th Reg't Wis. Vol
Camp near Corinth Sept 8th/62*

Dear Father & Mother,

I have not written [you] now for quite a little while. My last [one] was dated, I believe, Aug 31st. Since then I [have] rec'd two letters from you but it was not [my] fault that I did [not] answer them sooner, [the] same day that I rec'd the first one [we] rec'd orders to be in readiness to march at a moment's notice. We started about 3 o'clock in the afternoon with nothing on but our arms and equipments and two days provisions. We marched about ten miles that afternoon and evening in the direction of Kossuth and camped just outside of the town. We soon found out what we were out for, it was in search of Guirillas. Just before we got into Kossuth the scouts brought in word that the Guirillas were in considerable force just the other side of town. We pushed on as fast as possible and found rails laid across the road and in one place the road was fenced up completely. It did not take long however [to] remove all obstructions but we could not come up with the enemy. They had got too much the start of us.

The next day we marched nearly 30 miles in pursuit of them but it was useless; we could [not find] them. That night we camped [at a place] called Chewalla near the rail [road that] goes to Memphis. We staid in [camp] until nearly noon (long enough . . . to forage for something to eat) then we started back for camp. We arrived safe and sound with loss of one man from our Co. [and] having accomplished nothing. . . .

I have not time to write any more at present. . . . Your affectionate Son

J. K. Newton

Camp near Corinth Sept 22nd/62

Dear Parents:

I have just got back to camp where I found a letter from home waiting for me to read. You had better believe I read it the first thing and now the second thing to do is to answer it.

I suppose you will have heard before this time that Price has been routed again at Iucah Ala. Our Reg't was part of the detachment that was sent out in search of him. The Detachment was sent out under the command of Brig-Gen'l McArthur. There was another detachment sent out under Gen Ross, and another under Gen Rosencrans, and another under Gen Davis. They were all sent out for the purpose of dispersing Gen Price's command.[3]

We started from camp about five o'clock on Wednesday morning (the 17th inst.). It commenced to rain just about daylight, but that did not stop our going. We took an

---

[3] Confederate General Sterling Price was defeated at Iuka (which is actually in Mississippi) on September 19. Major-General William S. Rosecrans (whom Newton usually calls "Rosencrans") was in command of the District of Corinth; Brigadier-General Leonard Ross was in command of the Second Division under Rosecrans; Brigadier-General Jefferson C. Davis, of the Fourth.

easterly direction from Corinth and traveled until after dark. We then camped and went to sleep as well as we could in the rain. It rained all night and part of the next day. It then cleared away and we had pleasant weather all the rest of the time. We were gone just five days and we marched all day every day and one night until midnight so you can guess what kind of a time we had.

The third day out our Reg't and the 18th were sent out on a scouting expedition. We marched until about 3 o'clock in the afternoon through creeks and swamps before we saw anything suspicious. We were through a kind of plantation with Co's "B" & "D" as skirmishers. All at once we heard firing in front and we went ahead on the double quick and formed in line of battle ready to give it to them. The 18th was formed in line on the right of us and at right angles with us. When we formed in line the 18th thought that we were rebels and fired a few shots at us but they did no damage. One of them went so close to Capt Harrison that it singed his whiskers for him. As for the rebels they did not wait to fire the second round but they skedadled as fast as possible, leaving one man killed and five wounded, one fatally. Besides that we took five prisoners and about a dozen horses with all their equipments. The men were armed with doublebarreled shotguns and some with carbines.

After the skirmish we had to march until after dark to come up with our division. The next morning we heard heavy firing in the direction of Iucah and our Gen'l rec'd orders to march for that place as fast as possible to reinforce Gen'l Rosencrans. We reached that place about noon but the rebels did not wait for us. They retreated that morning about seven o'clock leaving their dead and wounded on the field. Our loss and theirs was about the same. One of the cavalry men told me that the union men and rebels lost about 300 men apiece in killed and wounded, whether it was so high as that or not I dont know.[4]

We did not go on the battlefield for we had only just got to the town when we got word that Price was working round in our rear to attack Corinth, so we had to make our way back as fast as possible. The news is now that Price thinks that the most of the men are out of Corinth scouting the country in search of him and he thinks that he can come right in here as easy as can be. I only hope he does think so for he will find us ready to receive him with all due honors. There is nearly 40 thousand men in Corinth now and I guess that is enough to whip him out. . . .

With love to all the family I

remain Your affectionate Son

J. K. Newton

Camp Near Corinth Sept 27/62

Dear Father & Mother:

I rec'd your very welcome letter this morning, and I intend to answer it now if I can but I dont know as I will be able to do it before I will be called to go to work again. I am at work in the cookhouse now and it keeps me busy I can tell you. We have had to give up every nigger that we had in camp to go to work on the breastworks that are being thrown up around Corinth. So we have to do our cooking ourselves again. . . . I dont know how long we will stay in Corinth. I should not wonder if we had to leave for Bolivar or *some other* place before long. . . .

---

[4] According to *Battles and Leaders,* II, 736, Union losses were 141 killed, 613 wounded, and 36 captured, a total of 790; Confederate losses were 85 killed, 410 wounded, and 40 captured, or a total of 535.

The boys are all well and hearty as usual and seem to be getting along first rate.

Your affectionate Son J. K. Newton

Benton Barracks St Louis Mo
Oct 29th, 62

Dear Father & Mother.

I have just got to a place where I can send a few lines home.

I have been running about all over "Secessia" for nearly a month and now I hope I can have a chance to rest a little. I suppose you have felt rather anxious about me since the battle of Corinth but I could not help it. I thought all along how I would like to send a few lines to you just to let you know that I was all right.

I was taken prisoner at Corinth on Friday afternoon. I suppose it will be enough at present to know that we are all right. Some other time I will give you all the particulars. We have been 11 days coming up the river from Vicksburg, where I was paroled, to St Louis where we arrived this forenoon. We have not been in the Barracks half an hour yet but I thought I would send a few lines home before I eat any thing. . . .

With love to all the family
I remain Your affectionate Son

J. K. Newton

Benton Barracks, St Louis Mo. Oct 31/62

My Dear Parents,

I have just got washed up nicely *once more,* so that I feel like a white man and now I am going to keep the promise that I made you in that hastily written note dated the 29th inst.—which I hope you have rec'd before this time—which was that I would give you an account of my "trials and tribulations" in the "land of the Secesh."

Well to begin at the beginning. On the 1st of Oct we rec'd orders to strike tents and pack up ready to move. In about an hour every thing was packed up, the wagons loaded, and we had three days rations in our haversacks. It was then about three o'clock in the afternoon. Col Oliver's Orderly rode up on the gallop and gave our Col some orders. Speculation began at once as to what they were, but we did not find out at once. We were ordered into line and marched off without a word. We took the road to Chewalla. When we got to the breastworks we were joined by the 18th Wis & 1st Minn battery.[5] We kept on and reached Chewalla about dark, having marched about ten miles. When we got out there we found that the pickets of the 15th Mich—which was stationed there—had been attacked and we had been sent to reinforce them. We were all of us pretty tired I can assure you. We were formed

---

[5] Chewalla is west of Corinth, and Colonel Oliver's Brigade—of which the 14th Wisconsin, under Colonel John Hancock, was a part —of Brigadier-General Thomas J. McKean's Division was ordered by Major-General Rosecrans on a scouting expedition to Chewalla. Newton's experience at Corinth consequently was one of constant retreating before superior forces. For an excellent description of the battle, see William S. Rosecrans, "The Battle of Corinth," in *Battles and Leaders,* II, 737–57.

in line of battle and the artillery placed in position and we laid down to get what rest we could, but they did not let us lay there long. We were roused up in about half an hour and marched back about half a mile where we took up another position. We lay there on our arms the rest of the night.

In the morning (Oct 2) about daylight the pickets began to fire and it began to rain about the same time. We secured our arms from the wet as well as we could and— waited. Pretty soon one of the scouts came in wounded and reported the enemy to be in force about two miles in front. In a few minutes the battery was limbered up and we were ordered to take up another position a little way to the rear. We did so. Had another skirmish, retreated again, and took up another position, and had *another* skirmish, and so we kept on all day, skirmishing and retreating until dark when we took up another position and kept it all night.

The next morning (Friday Oct 3) our skirmishers began to fire about seven o'clock. It soon turned out that the rebels were advancing on our position and the artillery opened on them. After they had fired a few shots our c/o was sent out to the right to relieve one of the other c/o's that was out there skirmishing. We went out almost half a mile on the doublequick, deployed out and lay down. Pretty soon we heard the rebels down in front of us, the officers giving orders, &c, but the men did not seem to obey them very willingly. At any rate they did not come on very fast. As soon as they came in sight we fired and *run*. The rebels ran too, but they ran away from *us,* as well as *we ran away from them.*

I ran back a few rods and stopped to look around me. The rebels were out of sight and hearing, and so was the c/o too. All of the boys that I could see were John Dollar,

John Ryan, and Tom Turriff,[6] so we all came together and talked the matter over. We agreed not to run until we saw something to run [from]. We acted wrong in that for the Capt had given orders to retreat but we were so far from him that we did not hear the order. We stayed there until the rebels came up again, and *then* we saw something to run for, and I can tell you we *did* run. We made for the place where we left the Reg't, when we got there the Reg't had left and we did not know whether they had gone back or forward. We concluded that *we would not go forward until we found out*—a wise conclusion wasn't it—

We went back more than a mile before we came in sight of any of our men. The ones we first came up to were cutting down a bridge to stop the advance of the enemy. We crossed the bridge just before it fell and made the best of our way back to our c/o. We had only just got in our places when we were ordered out to the left as skirmishers again. The Capt took command and placed us in what looked to be a pretty ticklish position, but it turned out to be just as good a place as could have been picked out. It was near the center of an open field. There was a rise in the center just high enough to protect us. We stood there until the enemy came up to the fense, when the Capt gave the command, "give it to 'em boys," and we blazed away and run. How the bullets did whistle about our ears as we ran. Our c/o never got together that day again.

When we got to where our Reg't made another stand about half of the c/o went to the left of the Reg't. I followed the Capt with ten or a dozen others and took our place on the right of the Reg't. We did not stay there long

---

[6] Dollar, of De Pere, was later discharged because of a wound he received in the battle; Ryan eventually became captain of the regiment and one of Newton's best friends; Turiff was also from De Pere.

when we were ordered out in front again with orders to
stand and fire whenever we saw an enemy and not to retreat until we rec'd orders. We went out in front about five
or six rods. The Reg't was placed just over the brow of a
hill and the battery in the road on top of the hill. We took
our positions each of us behind a tree and "waited for
'em." In a few minutes we could see them coming up the
road and the *battle* commenced. The cannon was fired over
our heads at the enemy, and *we* fired on our own hooks.
They charged on us once but we had the good luck to drive
them back. (I have heard since that Col Hancock gave
c/o "F" great praise for not running when the enemy
charged on us.)

It was not long before we could see the enemys skirmishers dodging from tree to tree and the bullets began to
fly again. Just then the order was given to "Rally on the
reserve" and we fell back to our places in the line. Where
our c/o lay in line we could not see the enemy as we were a
little below the brow of the hill, so we were ordered to the
front again. Capt Harrison *was* on *hand* and so was the
c/o but before we got to our old position the rebels
charged on us and the whole Reg't was driven back.

I could not run so fast as I had ought to on account of a
sore foot, and for one spell I was right between two fires. I
had sense enough left to know that such a thing would not
do for me so I went off to the left and as the Reg't fell back
the secesh went past me. I kept on and got over the abattis
and inside of the breastworks when on looking off to the
right I could see the enemy charge on the breastworks and
drive our men out. As soon as they gained the breastworks
they began to close in on my right so I made off more to the
left. I had gone about 40 rods when on looking through the
trees I could see the *"butternuts"* right in front of me. I
began to give up getting back to the Reg't then, but I

thought I would make the best of it so I lay down in the
ditch to see if they would not go past without seeing me,
but it was "no go." They were on both sides of the ditch
and when they came up—why I surrendered.

My gun and side arms were taken away but they did not
even search me. I thought it was strange at the time that
they did not take every thing that I had but I found out
very soon that if I stood up for my rights that I would come
out *all right*. So when one of them came up to me and told
me to give him my canteen I told him that I *could not
spare it*. The ones that I was taken prisoner by was a force
of cavalry, Villipigue in command.[7]

I was sent back to the rear along with a few others who
were taken near me. When I got to the rear I found a
number of men from our Reg't but only one other from
our c/o (I cant stop to correct grammatical mistakes so dont
expect it.) and that was John Ryan. Both of us came out
without a scratch. We lay down and listened to the roar of
the battle until the wounded began to be brought in and
then we had our hands full. We did not sleep much that
night I can tell you. There were about 20 of our Reg't
brought down where we were, some of them wounded
severely and others slightly. One of them died that night
and I helped to bury him. None of the wounded were from
our c/o.

About nine o'clock in the morning we were somewhat
surprised to hear the command given, "In retreat march.
Prisoners fall into line, doublequick," and away we all
went as fast as possible. I was then sure that Corinth was
safe.[8]

---

[7] Confederate General J. B. Villepigue.
[8] The Confederate retreat probably did not begin before two
o'clock in the afternoon.

We traveled all day as fast [as] we could walk, and at night we stopped about ten miles from the Hatchie River. It rained a little that night but that did not prevent our sleeping. The next morning we were started off at daylight, took the road to the Hatchie river. We were told that we were to be taken to Pocahontas, & from there we would be sent by rail to Vicksburg. We got in sight of the river just before noon when all at once we heard a cannon directly in front. We were halted and they began to send troops and artillery to the front. By that time I had come to the conclusion that their retreat was cut off and so it turned out to be. We were marched off to the left and placed in a ravine. We lay there about half an hour while the battle raged with fearfull distinctness in front. All at once a shell from one of our guns came crashing through the trees and exploded only a few rods from us. We did not wait for orders to march but skedadled as fast as possible while the shells were bursting all around us. The road was full of flying rebels so we had to go through the woods, guarded by a small force of cavalry.

As soon as we got out of range of our guns we were allowed to halt and rest a little. But the rebels were in full retreat and we were pushed on with the rest of them. We were taken a round about road and crossed the Hatchie about ten miles from where the battle was fought. We kept on until about midnight, when we were halted and a beef was killed for us. We built a few small fires and roasted it. This was the first thing they gave us to eat, and I can tell you it tasted good.

The next day we only marched 15 miles. We camped at Ripley. From there we marched to Holly Springs where we arrived on Thursday (Oct 9) about noon. We had a small piece of beef every night but the last one and there we got some sweet potatoes instead. From H. S. we went to Jackson by rail so we were better off in the traveling line, but no better as far as eating went. We got to Jackson about noon of the next day (10th). We were marched up town and placed in a square where a house had burnt down. We stayed there all the afternoon, and it rained all the time. After dark we were taken up to the state house and allowed to sleep in the halls and doorways wherever we could find a place.

In the morning (11th) we were placed on the cars again and taken to Vicksburg. The jail was filled up with part of us and the rest (180) were put into a sort of calaboose down near the river. I happened to be one of the last so I had to go into the calaboose. While we stayed there our rations consisted of half a pound of fresh beef & one pint of cornmeal to each man. Besides that we had some rice dealt out to us once, half a pint to each man. We had also a little sugar and a little molasses.

We were paroled on the 16th and on the 18th we were sent up the river under a flag of truce to one of our transports. . . . We got to St. Louis on the 29th and I guess we were about as ragged and dirty a set of wretches as one would wish to see. There was not one of us that did not have any quantity of *"graybacks"* as the Secesh call them.

Well I have got cleaned up and a new suit of clothes on, and now all that I ask is to go home for a little while. I feel just as though I could enjoy the comforts of home "for a season" with a good rest. . . .

Well I must close. I shall ever remain

Your Loving Son   J. K. Newton

Benton Barracks
Nov 13th/62

Dear Father & Mother:

I rec'd your welcome letter the 9th inst and you may be sure that I was glad to hear from you as it has been such a long time since I rec'd a letter from you. I suppose there must be a few letters for me at the camp but I have not rec'd them yet, I don't know what the reason is, either. I have had one letter from the reg't since I have been here and I am expecting another one every mail.

The letter that I got from the reg't mentioned Capt Harrisons death. I am sure that his death will be felt not only by our own co but by the whole Reg't, as well as by his family. There was not a better officer in the Reg't nor one who had more friends. I am afraid that our co will never get over his loss.

The Reg't is following up the rebels and is somewhere in the vicinity of Holly Springs now. They may have been in another battle before this time for all I know. The news this morning was that H. S. had been evacuated by the secesh and was now occupied by our forces. The report needs confirmation.- I can hardly think that the rebels would leave such a place as that is without a fight: to my mind it is the prettiest place in the "Southern Confederacy."

How I would like to be at home on thanksgiving day. I intend to if it is a possible thing, for I cant stay here. I am tempted every day to run the guard and get home the best way I can but then I think that without money I would be in a very poor plight indeed. For it would not do to lay around near St Louis to be picked up by the first patrol that comes along and without a person has money enough to pay their fare on the cars it is rather hard to get away.

I guess I might as well tell the whole story and done

with it. In the first place there is a set of Dutch officers
here over the Paroled Men and they dont intend to respect
our paroles in the least. Now, our paroles expressly forbids
our standing guard over any stores or prisoners, or doing
any fatigue duty, or *"any other duty generally performed
by soldiers."* Now I would like to know if that isn't strict
enough. But the officers set that aside and say that we have
got to stand guard, and do all kinds of fatigue duty or be
courtmartialed and run the risk of having one month's pay
stopped. When I came here and found how they were going
on I made up my mind to get away as soon as possible, but it
was not so easy as it might be, I soon found out, so I went
in the cookhouse, and now I am working as hard as I can
every day for nothing but to get rid of going in the guard-
house, for I *wont* break my parole. (I suppose you know
enough about me to know that I am obstinate about some
things when I once make up my mind.)

There is no chance for me to get my pay, for I cant get
my descriptive roll for the commander of the co is not at
Corinth to sign it and he may not be for a month yet.
There was a report that we were all going to be sent to
Prairie du Chien, but that has been knocked in the head
by Gov Salomon.[9]

They intend to keep us here all winter, *if they can,* for
they have no business to try to keep us in the first place.
Our paroles will pass us anywhere if we only have the
money to pay our passage.

If you feel as though you could get money enough together & send me 10 or 15 dollars I am sure I could earn it
again before I am exchanged. If I should not happen to I
suppose it would be a loss to you until I get paid again, but

---

[9] Prairie du Chien is in southwestern Wisconsin, on the Mississippi
River. Lieutenant-Governor Edward Salomon had become governor
of Wisconsin in April of 1862, after the death of Louis P. Harvey.

when that will be, as I said before, I cant tell. I dont want you to put your self out about it, just act as you think best. . . .

With Love to all the family, I remain, Your Son

J. K. Newton

Mr. Newton did send James some money, and he went home for a short vacation. By the middle of December he was back in camp, at Madison, Wisconsin.

Madison
Camp Randall, Dec. 13th/62

Dear Father & Mother:

I arrived in camp on thursday night, and I would have written to you yesterday but I did not have any paper or stamps so I went down town yesterday and now I have both and I can write as often as I please.

I got to Milton Junction [10] thursday morning at five o'clock. I had to wait there until two o'clock in the after [noon] so that I did not get to Madison until dark. The camp is about 2 miles south west of the city near the college.[11] It is a very pretty place in summer I should think but just now it is rather muddy. It rained quite hard all day yesterday, and today it is blowing like everything from the southwest and it is freezing a little too, I should not

---

[10] Milton Junction is a town southeast of Madison.

[11] Camp Randall was later incorporated into the city limits of Madison. The "college" to which Newton refers is the University of Wisconsin.

wonder if we should have a fall of snow before the weather changes.

Yesterday the drafted men were mustered into the U. S. Service, there are some pretty goodlooking men among them, but as a general thing they aint much to brag of. They have been fighting and raising cain generally, ever since they have been here. There are about 30 paroled men here, all but nine of them belong to the 1st Wis. Cav.

Besides the 1st Cav. there are three here who belong to the 14th, five to the 8th, and one to the 16th, so that we have a large enough squad to be sent to the Reg't already.

We expect to be sent off on Monday. I hope we will too for I am sure I dont want to stay here any longer than I can possibly help. Still it is just as the commanding officer says. We are in very comfortable quarters, and have plenty to eat, and we can get a pass whenever we want it, so you see we aint so very bad off after all. I guess we can manage to stand it for a little while. . . .

I have been over to see the cannon that was taken by the 14th at Pittsburg.[12] It looks as "natural as life." The spike has never been taken out; except the engraving, it is just the same as we sent it home. . . .

I remain Your affectionate Son,

James

Camp Randall, Madison
Dec 24th 1862

Dear Father & Mother;

I am here in Madison still but it looks more like my leaving now, than it has before while I have been here.

---

[12] These cannon still stand at Camp Randall in Madison.

. . . I guess if we get off by monday we will be lucky. I dont see what they are keeping us here for, when we are exchanged. I haven't done a thing since I came here but just eat and sleep and run around town. If we could not get passes every day I dont know what I would do. I am afraid I could not stand it long. As it is I spend most of my time in the library of the State Historical Society.

I guess I would not have had so many things to take along with me for the boys if the folks in Depere had known that I would have stayed here so long. The letters that I have will be old enough I guess before they get them, but "I'll bet" they will be acceptable for all that. . . .

With love to all the family I remain
Your affectionate Son.

James

Fort Pickering Memphis
January 5th, 1863

My Dear Parents:

When I wrote to you last I was at Madison with no prospect of leaving very soon, but I got away sooner than I expected to. . . .

We got to Cairo thursday afternoon and were sent on board a transport at once and started down the river. We arrived at Memphis on Saturday (Jan. 3) morning and were sent right up to the Fort to wait until a train can be sent through to Holly Springs when we will be sent to the Reg't. The report is that our Reg't is guarding the railroad out near Holly Springs. . . .

I suppose you have heard before this time that they have

been fighting down to Vicksburg for several days. Yesterday morning the report was that Banks had failed to "come to time" and consequently we had been badly whipped there, but last night a boat came up the river bringing the news that Vicksburg was ours with 40,000 prisoners. No doubt that is exagerated but I guess we can believe a good part of it.[13] There has been some desperate fighting down there any way, and if we have gained the victory it has been a great victory. On the other hand if we have been defeated, it has been a great defeat. They have been fighting for about ten days already and I dont know how much longer they will fight. . . .

Your affectionate Son

James

---

[13] Major-General Nathaniel P. Banks did not arrive, and Major-General William T. Sherman failed to carry Vicksburg, losing over 2,000 men at Chickasaw Bluffs, while the Confederate losses were about 200. See George W. Morgan, "The Assault on Chickasaw Bluffs," *Battles and Leaders,* III, 467–69.

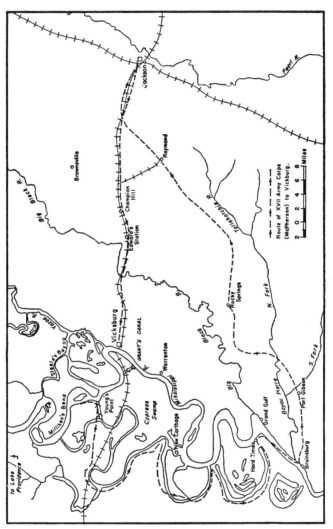

Vicksburg area

CHAPTER FOUR

THE
VICKSBURG WINTER

Camp near Memphis, Jan 16th, 1863

My Dear Parents

It has been a long time since I wrote to you last, but I suppose you know what to lay it to. When I wrote last I was in the Fort at Memphis. I left there a few days after for the Reg't. They were camped then at Moscow. I got there the day before they were ordered to leave there for Memphis. . . .

We were ordered to leave for down the river this morning. The order read, "prepare to go immediately with three days cooked rations in haversacks," but for all that I guess we wont go before tomorrow or the day after. . . .

Our destination undoubtedly is Vicksburg. They have been fighting considerable down there but it seems they cant take the city until the old 14th goes down to help them. There is hardly any sickness in the Reg't now as

51

the boys say: "it has simmered down to the tough ones." I think myself that those that are left can be depended on.

We are camped about half a mile outside of the city. We were in hopes that we would be allowed to stay here all winter but it seems they think too much of McArthurs Division to allow them to lay still long. . . .

I have been staying in the same tent with Mr Wheeler and Oscar Cooley since I got back. They intend to have me act as co. clerk . . .

Give my respects to all inquiring friends. With Love to all the family I remain

Your affectionate Son

James

Steamer St Louis at Gains Landing
Saturday January 24th, 1863

My Dear Parents,

When I wrote you last we were about starting from Memphis for *somewhere else,* but where we did not know then, but we have found out since. We are within twelve miles of Vicksburg, just above "Millikins Bend," and I suppose we are to cut across the country to the river below Vicksburg to open communication with Gen Banks and also to keep the rebels from skedadling into Louisiana. We got here yesterday afternoon but the troops have not landed yet and I dont know when we will. Probably we will be kept on board until they have something for us to do. They detail a Reg't every day to work on the canal.[1] It may come our turn pretty soon.

---

[1] The canal was being dug by the Union troops in an attempt— eventually unsuccessful—to reroute the Mississippi River in order to

There was quite a little fight yesterday forenoon right in front of Vicksburg, just where the railroad crosses the canal. There was one Colonel killed besides fifteen men. I have not heard what the name of the Col was.

Today we have heard several "big guns" down to Vicksburg but I have not heard what it was all about yet. Yesterday Gen McArthur went down on the "Platte Valley" within sight of Vicksburg, and the secesh threw a shell at the boat, but it fell half a mile short. However he concluded that he had gone *quite far enough,* so he turned round and came back. I suppose they intend to make a sure thing of it this time before they try to take Vicksburg again.

There was two men deserted from our Co when we left Memphis. There names were John Tillmans [2] and John McLymans. The last one was no loss to the Co though, for he was as great a coward as ever lived. When we went into the battle of Corinth he pretended to be sick but he did not get any sympathy from any of the boys.

I have just heard what the firing was for today. Gen McArthur and Col Ransom (the commander of our Brigade) [3] made a reconnoissance in force opposite the city. They fired at one of the Secesh transports, and the secesh threw several shells at them but no one was hurt. . . .

When you hear that Vicksburg has been taken you may

---

by-pass the batteries at Vicksburg. For a description of these and other attempts, see Ulysses S. Grant, "The Vicksburg Campaign," in *Battles and Leaders,* III, 493–539.

[2] Tilliman returned to the company and was killed in action charging Vicksburg, May 22, 1863.

[3] Brigadier-General Thomas E. G. Ransom of the Second Brigade of General John McArthur's Sixth Division of General James B. McPherson's Seventeenth Army Corps.

make up your mind that the 14th has had something to do with it. Give my resp'ts to all inquiring friends.

Your Affectionate Son, James

Behind the LEVEE
Somewhere in Louisiana
Feb 5th 1863

Dear Father & Mother

. . . When I wrote to you last we were aboard the steamer, I believe. I dont recollect writing to you since. We left the boat a week ago last Sunday (Jan 26) and camped inside the Levee and we have been here ever since. *Taking Vicksburg,* I suppose.

It rained all day yesterday and the river has been rising very rapidly for several days so I guess you have had your share of rain up north. If the water rises much more we will have to *evacuate* this place in a hurry, for the Levee is washed away about a mile below here and I expect to see the land flooded in a few days. . . .

Last Sunday morning the Ram "Queen of the West" ran down past Vicksburg. The Rebels fired one hundred & eleven shots at her as she passed the batteries but although she is only a wooden boat she was not damaged in the least. Only four shots struck her, two of them 64 pounders. As the Ram passed by the city the steamer Vicksburg was lying at the Levee and it was such a good chance that they stopped and ran into her twice, and then kept on down the river. The steamer sunk down to her guards before they got out of sight.

It seems to me if the wooden boats can run down past the batteries, that there is no need of cutting the canal for the gunboats, but they keep on digging. Gen Grant says now he has commenced that he is bound to have the gunboats go through there by spring. . . .

We have had real nice weather for winter since we have been here, although sometimes when it rains it is rather disagreeable. Give my respects to all inquiring friends and dont forget to write often. . . .

I remain your Affectionate Son

James

Headquarters 14th Wis Vol Infy
Lake Providence, La. Feb 13th/63

Dear Father & Mother

. . . When I wrote last we were in camp near Vicksburg. We broke camp the day after I wrote and moved on to the boats. We steamed up the river to a little town called Providence and then marched back into the country about five miles and camped on the shore of as pretty a lake as ever was made. It is about eight miles long and one mile wide and the water is as clear as chrystal. Quite a contrast to the *Miss* river I can tell you.

The object of sending our Division up here is to cut a canal from the Miss into Lake Providence, and from there into Bayou Macon which empties into the Miss a few miles below Natches. In that way we will get around Vicksburg before they know it.

There are several Rebel transports in the Wachita [4] river that are afraid to run down on account of the Ram "Queen of the West" which run past Vicksburg a little

---

[4] The Ouachita River; this is the spelling Newton habitually uses.

while ago. The day after she run down, she burnt three Rebel boats loaded with stores and provisions for the Rebels.

The canal from the river into the Lake will be 80 rods long with ten feet fall. If we dont empty the *Miss* into Lake Providence when we get the canal dug it will be a wonder to me. I guess we will make a big thing of it, big enough to make the Rebs stare some. The only wonder to me is that it was not thought of before.

The Levee in front of the town is about twenty feet high. I'll bet we'll make the citizens evacuate in a little while. There is a awful waste of property attends our army wherever it goes but we dont think so much of it as we would if it was our own property that we were wasting. . . . I should not wonder if they would try to drive us away from here before long but McArthurs men are enough for several thousands of them.

I cant afford to write many more letters unless I get an answer to some of them pretty soon. Love to all the family

Yours affectionately

James

In February James was appointed Company Clerk.

Lake Providence, La.
February 28th, 1863

Dear Father and Mother.

I have not written to you for several days and I guess its about time I did so. . . . The canal from the river to the lake is almost finished now, but they dont intend to let the water in until the Bayou is cleared out. They are carrying a small Tug—with machinery rigged somehow to cut trees and stumps under water—from the river to the lake so that they can clear out the Bayou in a hurry when they once get at it. There are about two hundred niggers at work on the canal now and more coming in every day.

I hope you will write as soon as you receive this if you dont before and be sure and write all the news. . . .

Your Affectionate Son

J. K. Newton

Head Qrs 14 Wis Vols.
Lake Providence, La.
Saturday, March 7/63

Dear Father and Mother:

I am sure you cant say that I dont write to you often. . . .

We had quite a holiday a few days ago. Our Brigade was inspected and Col. Ransom (our Brigadier) offered a reward of $15.00 to the co that made the best appearance on inspection. One of the co's in our Reg't was awarded the prize but we have not found out which one it is yet. Maj Strong [5] (who kicked up such a fuss with the Rebels one time down on the Potomac) was the inspecting officer. He had not one word of fault to find with our co. He told the Col of the 17th that he had a fine lot of boys and that was all he could say for them.

There is a little Tug running up and down the lake now. They brought it over from the river by some means

---

[5] Possibly Major William E. Strong of the Twelfth Wisconsin.

or other. I did not go down to see how it was done. It will
be a great help as a means of transportation up & down the
Bayou as fast as they get it cleared out. It created quite a
sensation I can tell you when it first steamed up the lake.
There is considerable talk of our leaving here soon but
I dont know how true it is. For my part if we have got to
spend the summer down south as far as this I would rather
stay here than go anywhere else.

Our c/o signed the payrolls yesterday for two months
pay from the last of Aug. to the last of Oct. They would
not let Pat Martin & I sign them because we were not here
to muster [6] so you see we will not get any pay this time
nor the next either for we were absent from two musters.
So you see when I do get any pay it will be six months altogether. Well all I can say is that it will be first rate when
it does come. . . . Love to all the family

Your Affectionate Son

J. K. Newton

Head Q'rs 14 Wis Vol
Lake Providence, La.
Thursday March 12/63

My Dear Parents:

When I wrote you last I did not expect to get paid when
the rest of the boys were, but I was very happily disappointed for I rec'd two months pay today with the rest of
the Co. The Paymaster took a certificate from the Capt in
lieu of my muster for pay. I never saw it done before, but
I am very well satisfied that it is so for it gives me the

---

[6] Martin had been a deserter for a short period, and Newton, of
course, had been captured.

pleasure of sending a little money home this time. And I
know you must be in need of it. I sent twenty ($20⁰⁰) dol-
lars by express today along with several of the other
boys. . . .

I expected to get a letter from you today when the mail
came in but I was disappointed *as usual.* . . . My health is
first rate at present. In fact all the Boys are enjoying good
health. I have not time to write any more. Give my respects
to all inquiring friends

With love to all the family I remain

Your Affectionate Son

J. K. Newton

Head Q'rs 14 Reg't Wis Vols
Lake Providence Apr 1st/63

Dear Father & Mother.

. . . Two weeks ago last monday night (Mch 15) we
were ordered to get ready to march in fifteen minutes
without tents or baggage. We packed up and started in
that time and did not get back again until yesterday. Our
letters were forwarded to us, so that we had the pleasure of
reading, but not of answering them.

It was dark before we reached the town of Providence
(after leaving our camp) but when we got within half a
mile of there we heard an awful roaring in front and pretty
soon the water began to rush by us in the canal to the lake.
We came to the conclusion that the water had been let in
from the river and sure enough when we got there we
found it so. There had been a small cut made in the Levee
and the water was wearing it away slowly, but surely.

The day after we left the water was rising so fast in the
Lake that they had to move our camps nearer the river and

in a few days the water drove them out again, and they went up the river a few miles. Just before we came back the camp was moved again and now we are camped about 3 miles below the town just behind the Levee.

While all this moving was going on we were up the river about 50 miles hunting after cotton. We found between 3 & 4000 bales, hauled it to the river and shipped it down to Vicksburg to use on the Gun boats (at least so we were told). I think our two weeks trip paid pretty well. (Some one will get the good of it but I dont believe that one will be Uncle Sam.) Calling the cotton worth 80 cts pr pound what we got while we were gone would amount to more than one million and a half of dollars. If we keep on in this way I guess they can afford to pay us up pretty soon. . . .

I must close. Give my respects to all the folks at Depere With Love to all the family I remain

Your affectionate son James

Head Q'rs 14th Wis Infy Vols
Lake Providence April 10th/63

My Dear Parents

I rec'd yours of March 24th several days ago. . . . We had a grand review three days ago. The reviewing officer, was Adj: Gen: Thomas, from Washington, Adj: Gen: of the United States. After the review was over there were several speeches delivered, by the Adj: Gen: and Generals McPherson, McArthur, Col Crocker, of the 16th Iowa, and several others.[7]

---

[7] Brigadier-General Lorenzo Thomas served as adjutant general from May of 1861 until the spring of 1863. Colonel Marcellus M. Crocker was in command of the Third Brigade of the Sixth Division.

The principal subject discussed, was the policy, at last determined on by the President, of calling into the service Negro Reg'ts, commanded by officers selected from the Reg'ts now in the field.[8] The Adj: Gen: said, "that he was authorized by the President to commission all such men selected and that he would just as soon give a commission as Capt to a private as any one else if he was only capable": he also said, "that he was authorized to call into the servise as many Negro Reg'ts as he saw fit in the southwest, he had already organized two Reg'ts at Helena, and he wanted to organize two more down here, and take all of the officers from the 6th Division."

When the Adj: Gen: sat down, some one called out, "McArthur." The whole Div. took up the cry and for a few moments nothing else could be heard but, "McArthur, McArthur." At last he rose and took the stand, when such a cheer as burst forth I am sure, has not been heard for some time in the entire south: for more than five minutes it was one continued cheer. It gratified him, I know by his looks. He said, "It gratified him to learn that the President had at last decided on a settled policy in regard to this matter; that he, as a soldier, was determined to carry out the views of the government, whatever they were; but that he would always show more alacrity, in the cause when it was in consonance with his own feelings; and such he felt to be the case now."

After McArthur sat down a man—Capt Chirk by name —was called to the stand; he spoke for nearly an hour. I am sure I would like nothing better than to see his speech in print; he began by saying "that nothing was farther from

---

[8] There had been a bitter fight in the North on the advisability of allowing Negroes to serve as troops. Early in 1863 Lincoln decided to use colored troops, serving under white officers, on a segregated basis.

his thoughts than that he would be called upon to speak, he felt that after listening to the gentlemen before him he could not make a speech, in fact what he should say, he wanted us to take as an *exhortation after the regular sermon.*" Speaking of the resources of the United States he said: "I have heard the opinion expressed in some portions of the army, that we could not whip the south; now I want to know the reason why: we have men enough, we have rations enough, we have guns enough, we have greenbacks enough, and I wish the Adj: Gen'l to understand that *we have greybacks enough.*" (That brought down the house I can tell you.) Just before he sat down he said, "that he had been thinking of applying for a commission as Col. of one of the Nigger Regts and he wanted all who were in favor of his getting it to say, "Aye." (A unanimous "Aye" burst from the crowd.) Contrary "No," (there was "Nary No,") "Carried unanimously" said he and sat down. The Adj: Gen: rose and said that he should have to give him the commission.[9] He brought it in just in the right time, and I would advise any-one who desires promotion to "go and do likewise." . . .

Ever your Affectionate Son

James

HeadQ'rs 14th Wis Vol Infy
Lake Providence April 18th 1863

Dear Father and Mother
    . . . We had a Division review yesterday, and another one today. Gen McArthur was the reviewing officer. He

---

[9] This officer has not been positively identified. Newton may have miswritten the name of Captain James C. Clark, who became lieu-

complimented the 14th very highly on their appearance today. In fact the 14th was the best drilled, best dressed, best marching, and by all means the *best looking* Reg't on review. I am not alone in my opinion for the commander of the Brigade calls the 14th one of his *"old standbys."* Well we have earned our reputation, and although it has cost us something and may cost us some of our best men yet, still I think it will pay to keep it up, cost what it will. The crisis seems to be approaching, in regard to the taking of Vicksburg, and as we are within striking distance, we will not be left out when the time comes to take it.

Night before last, the camp was aroused by some of the heaviest firing that we have yet heard. It seemed to shake the ground here, and we are full thirty miles in a strait line from Vicksburg. We did not know what was up at the time but we found out last night. It seems that the troops below Vicksburg are in need of transports, (though I dont know what use they are going to put them to) and night before last Gen Grant *sent some down to them.* Three Gunboats and eight Transports started together to run down stream past Vicksburg. The boats were protected by barges loaded with cotton, and although it retarded their speed considerable, yet none of them were willing to go without such protection. The gunboats and six transports went by unhurt; one transport was set on fire by a shell and burnt, and one other was disabled; on the whole I think they came out first rate.

The Yazoo Expedition did not amount to much. They had to burn a number of their boats and crowd the men on the rest in order to get back into the Miss: river again; the boats passed by here a few days ago. The men were a

tenant colonel of the Seventh Regiment, Corps d'Afrique, organized at Port Hudson, Louisiana, in the summer of 1863.

sorry looking set, I can tell you, more than one third of them were sick and the rest so dirty as to be hardly recognizable. It dont improve, either the looks or the health of any lot of men to be on board a boat two months, and especially such boats as those were. The smoke stacks, and escape pipes had to be cut down nearly to the deck, so as to clear the trees as they went under them; and no man on board could keep clear of the smoke. They were a hard looking set when they went by here. They are going down so as to be on hand at the taking of Vicksburg. They seem to think that if they could not get into the rear, they stand a good chance of getting into the front of the "old Slaughter house." (The name Vicksburg goes by.) [10]

Give my respects to all the good people of Depere, and dont forget to write often.

Your affectionate Son,

James K. Newton

Head Q'rs 14th Reg't Wis Vol Infy
Camp on Smith's Plantation, near Carthage, La.
Thursday April 30th 1863

My Dear Parents:

The Reg't has moved again as you will see by looking at the date of this. We left Millikins Bend last Sunday (April 26) afternoon and after a very tiresome march arrived here "safe and sound" (but covered with mud from head to

---

[10] For an account of Sherman's ill-fated attempt to get into the rear of Vicksburg, see Earl Schenck Miers, *The Web of Victory, Grant at Vicksburg* (New York, 1955), pp. 116–30. Miers's book is also a good source for the entire campaign.

foot) yesterday April 29 afternoon. I rec'd your letter dated April 14 day before yesterday. We were then at Richmond —the little town where some of our boys had that little fight last February—and you may be sure that I did not feel much like answering it then even if I had pen and paper handy, for we had been two days on the march then, through mud up to our knees.

It commenced to rain the same day we started (to punish us I suppose for marching on Sunday) and it rained two days steady. When you remember that the country down here is perfectly flat with no hills whatever—unless you call the Levee a hill—you can *partly* imagine what kind of walking it must be. Our Reg't was rear guard the first two days. Nice times it was (for young ducks) helping the teams through the mud whenever they got set which was pretty often, I can tell you.

It was the first march that I ever went on and carried my knapsack. I dreaded it considerable at first but I soon found that I could carry it first rate. After the first day it didnt bother me in the least. . . .

There is some hot work going on near Vicksburg, the big guns have been "talking" all day: and now every little while I can hear a "sullen roar" which says that the fighting isn't over with. I hope to hear in a few days what is up. The head men down here seem to take it for granted that Vicksburg will be evacuated before we can get around in the rear, and cut off their retreat. It's the only thing that can save *them,* but it would be too bad to let them get away so easy. It seems to me as though that bridge might have been burnt long before this if they had tried very hard, but I am in hopes that things will come out all right in the end.

Matters seem to be coming to a crisis both in the eastern and western and also in Tenn army, and if they only turn

out as we all hope they will the war will soon come to an
end. And then "hurrah for home." If we dont make the
wood ring it won't be our fault, but hold on, Vicksburg
aint taken yet, I almost got ahead of my time. . . .

Your dutiful Son

James Newton

HeadQuarters 14 Wis: Vol: Infy
Camp on Smith's Plantation, Near
Carthage, La. Sunday, May 10th 1863

Dear Father, Mother
& *all the rest of the family*
    . . . There is some prospect now of our moving from
this place though where we will go I dont know. I think
though that we will keep on to the rear of Vicksburg.

Yesterday the news came from Carthage that Gen Logans
Div had swung round into Jackson and taken the city. The
report is not confirmed yet. Logan's Div belongs to our
Army Corps. It has always been kept in the reserve until
lately and there is no telling what Logan may try to do.
He has considerable ambition and I should not wonder if
he would try to work around Sherman in some way and
get the credit of taking Vicksburg himself. Well as long
as it is taken I dont care who has the credit of taking it.[11]
If our Brigade starts from here soon enough I should not
wonder if we would have a finger in the pie. The officers
have been notified that they had better lay in ten days provisions and get themselves in readiness for a march at a

---

[11] The rumor was untrue. General Sherman and General John A.
Logan both entered Jackson on the same day, May 14, 1863.

moments notice; that looks as though we wouldn't stay here long. In fact I would not wonder if we would start today; we have hardly been on a march while we have been down here that we did not start on Sunday. . . .

With love to all I remain

Your affectionate Son

James K. N.

P.S. The order has come. We are to march at one o'clock to day. Well it cant be helped so here goes for packing up.

James

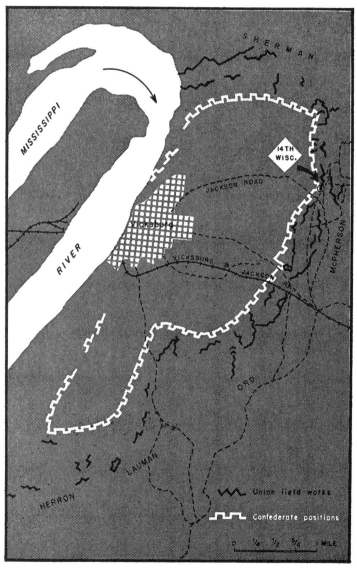

Siege of Vicksburg

CHAPTER FIVE

THE SIEGE
OF VICKSBURG

H'd Q'rs 14th Wis Vols Near Vicksburg
May 24th 1863

My Dear Parents

I hardly know how to begin this letter, I have so much to tell and so little time to tell it in. You must have heard before this of the unsuccessful charge we made a few days ago on one of the forts near Vicksburg, but I suppose you have not heard any of the particulars. I got permission to come down to the Hospital from the front on purpose to write you a few lines to Depere to relieve you from the suspense which I know you must feel on our acc't.

Our Co suffered pretty severely. Both Lieuts wounded, our Capt hurt by a fall down hill. Every Sergt wounded, and all but one Corporal wounded.[1] The Corpl who is un-

---

[1] Company F saw eighteen men wounded and five killed during Grant's second unsuccessful attempt to assault the fortifications of

hurt is Tom Stewart. He was detailed as sharpshooter the day before and did not go into the charge. I have been acting orderly Serg't since the rest were wounded and expect to act as such until McFarland gets back or at least till one of the Sergts get round again.

There is bad news for Mr Leroys folks but I hope you will make it as easy for them as you can. John is among the missing but whether he is killed or wounded I dont know. We have hunted for him as near the fort as we dare to go but with no success. All I can hope for is that he is wounded and has been picked up and carried to some other Hospital. I will enclose a copy of the report sent in to the Regimental H'dQrs. and the wounded boys want you to send it round so that there friends will not worry on their accounts. Hardly any of them are able to write and otherwise it would be a long time before their folks would hear from them.

How I came off the field with out being wounded with the rest I am sure I cant tell. The nearest that I came to being wounded was when a ball went through the rim of my hat slightly brushing my forehead.

There is not much news only that we have the rebels in a pretty tight place. They are completely surrounded and if we cant make them surrender any other way we can starve them out.

I almost forgot to mention John Sullivan, he was very badly wounded in the arm and it had to be taken off. He worries about it a good deal because he will never be able to help his father any more.

Love to all,

Your Son James

Vicksburg, May 22, 1863. The brigade lost 57 men killed, 275 wounded, and 32 captured, or a total of 364. This was by far the heaviest loss suffered by Company F during the war.

Head Q'rs 14th Wis
Near Vicksburg, May 29th/63

Dear Mother;

. . . We are still camped in the ravine where we were when I wrote last.[2] They have given up taking Vicksburg by storm, and we are now besieging it. Sharpshooters are detailed every day, who creep as near the enemy's works as possible and pick off every one who shows his head above the breastworks. The enemy is not damaged much by them however: it seems to scare them more than any thing else.

Our Artillery does not seem to do them much damage either only to knock down their breastworks and they can build them up as fast as we can knock them down. Sometimes neither side will fire more than two or three cannon shots all day and as like as not the next day there will be a continual roar for hours together, which even shakes the ground and keeps up such a din that we can hardly "hear ourselves think."

Last night there was a "fatigue party" of 40 men detailed from our Reg't to build breastworks; and there was a rumor that the city was going to be bombarded from all quarters in the morning. Of course we all expected pretty lively times in the morning, especially when we heard that the fatigue party was to build a fort in a better position, one from which they would be able to rake the enemy's breastworks in a manner that would occasion them some surprise. Well this morning sure enough the ball commenced, and—what was somewhat strange—the Rebels commenced it by firing the first shot; however our batteries soon silenced them, and then kept up such a roar for an hour or so as is seldom heard and when once heard is never forgotten. As our Col expressed it, "it was the biggest

---

[2] The letter is lost.

fourth of July that I ever saw." While our batteries were using up the enemys breastworks in the rear, the gun boats and mortars in front were throwing shells into the "devoted city," so on the whole I guess they had their hands full. I cant pity the rebels themselves but it does seem too bad for the women and children in the city.

In the night when it is still and quiet, I often go up on the hill and watch the mortarboats throwing shells into the city; at such times I can distinctly hear the shells crash through the houses. Indeed, some of the boys went so far as to say that they could hear the screams of women and children, but—their *ears must have been better than mine.*

The position of the fort which our Reg't helped to build last night turned out to be right on top of the hill, directly in the rear of the ravine in which we are encamped. The shot from that battery went directly over our heads. Although not dangerous in the least to be in front of the cannon while they are firing, I assure you it is very disagreeable, for the concussion of the air is very sensibly to be felt, almost crushing a person to the ground. . . .

There was a cessation of hostilities for a couple of hours the other day to enable each party to bury their dead. . . . The "Rebs" were quite friendly to us while the white flag was up. They came out of their entrenchments and we went out of ours and met them down in the ravine which separates their breastworks from ours. We had a long talk over matters and things in general. They agreed with us perfectly on one thing. If the settlement of this war was left to the Enlisted men of both sides we would soon go home. I think they were about right, dont you? . . .

The idea you seem to have about Edward, dear Mother, is, I think, hardly the right one. You seem to take it for granted that he could either come home discharged, or on furlough, if he only wanted to. Now I want you to recollect that there never was so hard a time to get out of the service since the war commenced as now. There are several men in our Co who really ought to be discharged, but it is of no use for them to try, the "head men" *will not* discharge them. Unless a person has been wounded in the service and unfitted by that means it is almost entirely useless for them to ask for a discharge. As for a furlough hardly any sane man would ask for one, for he would be sure to be disappointed. You may think that I am exaggerating affairs a little but it is not so, for I am speaking what I know to be true as far as relates to the Dep't of the *Miss;* and I have it from pretty good sources that it is the same all through the western Dep't. There is no doubt but what Edward had *ought* to go home awhile to recruit his health, but I think if he would try, he would find it almost impossible to get leave. . . .

How strange it would look to see the trees just beginning to "leave out." Why! down here the trees have been green for more than three months. We have ripe plums, blackberries, &c. The Peaches, Pears, and Apples are almost ripe too. But for all that I would never live down here, for what is the south compared with the good old north. In my estimation the south would suffer some by the comparison.

You say dear Mother that I never told you whether I found my testament or not when I returned to the Reg't. I did get it, I am happy to say. And it was almost the only thing that was saved for me, I lost almost everything. It has cost me almost twenty five dollars to replace the different articles of Clothing and other miscellaneous articles, of little value it is true, when taken by themselves, and yet it is hard to get along without them.

You say in your letter that you wrote with strange feelings not knowing whether I would ever read what you wrote or not. I also while I write am thinking of the uncertainty of human life. How can I think otherwise, with the sound of battle all round me. And yet if God should call me from this world into the next, I hope that he will so strengthen you that you can say with Job "the Lord gave and the Lord taketh away, blessed be his holy name."

I have long been under deep concern for my sins, but I have learned to put my trust in God believing that he will blot them all out of the "book of his remembrance" if sincerely repented of. I hope and trust that God will forgive all my sins for the sake of Jesus Christ our Redeemer, but I have not that clear, bright evidence that my sins are forgiven me, that I so much desire. Oh! My Mother pray for me, that God will keep me from the many temptations to which I am exposed. I presume you have often heard of the vices of the camp, but you did not realize it. No person can ever realize it until they have been placed in some such a position as I am now, and then they will begin to realize what is meant by the vices of the camp; then they will see all kinds of iniquity openly practiced without being reproved by any one. . . .

I am still acting as Orderly and expect to for some time yet. Love to all the family.

Yours Affectionately: James

In the Field Before Vicksburg, Miss
Friday June 5th 1863

My Dear Father

I rec'd your welcome letter last night and I hasten to reply. Knowing as I do that your anxiety must be very great on my account while the siege of Vicksburg is progressing.

I am enjoying first rate health. I have nothing to com-

plain of in the least unless I except the fact that I am
getting *ragged and lousy* with the rest, but as soon as Vicksburg is taken we will get over that in a jiffy.

The weather is very pleasant, although quite hot; that
dont bother us much however, for most of the fatigue work
is done at night, when our men are out of sight of the rebel
sharpshooters. Our men are now engaged in planting a
battery of heavy siege guns on a hill within 400 yards of
the enemys line of breastworks. When it is ready to open
on them I expect to see some *tall skedadling.*

Night before last we were called up at two oclock and
lay in line of Battle until morning expecting the rebels
would *make a break* somewhere along our line and try to
cut their way out. There was no attempt made in our
front, but several miles to the left heavy fighting was heard
all night: what the cause of it was I have not yet heard.

All was quiet on the rebels side last night; on our side
the heaviest batteries along the line, together with the
mortar boats in front, kept up a continual cannonading,
throwing shells in to the heart of the city; they have perfect range, and can throw shell at night exactly as well as
they can in the day time.

It is a pretty sight I can tell you, to see the shells from
the mortars going up higher and higher until they look
as though they were clear up among the stars; and then to
see them begin to fall, going faster and faster as they near
the ground. Some of them burst high in the air scattering
pieces of shell in every direction and without doubt deal-
ing death to the inhabitants: others do not burst until after
they strike, and then we can hear the crash as the shell
goes down through the houses very plainly.

Three nights ago the city was set on fire by the bursting
of a shell: from where I stood on the hill I could distinctly
hear the firebells ringing the alarm. Our batteries were in-

stantly turned in the direction of the fire, and shot and shell rained thick and fast on that portion of the city— which, without doubt, effectually prevented the gathering of a very large crowd to put out the fire. It was still burning at noon of the next day.[3]

Our pickets are getting to be quite sociable with those of the enemy: it is quite a common occurrance for them to meet half way without arms to drink a cup of coffee together, and have a long talk over matters and things in general. It very often happens too that the rebels do not go back again, preferring to stop with our men until they can be sent north.

I am glad to hear that the crops are doing so finely. If any of them should fail I dont know what you would do, for it must cost considerable to live nowadays up north, more than it has ever done before. You say the fruit trees are all in blossom up north. It would look odd to me to see trees in bloom down here now, I can tell you. The plums, Cherries, and Blackberries have been ripe for quite a while. Blackberries especially are very plenty. . . .

I am sure I would like to meet you at the station as well as you would like to have me. I have had a very polite invitation to spend the 4th of July in Depere, but I had to decline it on account of other *pressing business.* I hope to be able to spend the next one at home. . . .

I must close hoping that you will write often. Love to all the family.

Your Affectionate Son

James

---

[3] For an excellent account of life in the city itself, see Peter F. Walker, *Vicksburg, A People at War, 1860–1865* (Chapel Hill, 1960), pp. 93–201.

Head Quarters 14th Wis Vols
In the Rear of Vicksburg June 27/63

My Dear Mother.

. . . Our Reg't was paid off a few days ago. As soon as possible I shall send some money home. I dont like to trust it in the mail, when it is so irregular as it is at the present time.

Since we were paid off a person cannot go five rods in any part of our camp without seeing someone gambling. The day after we were paid there were a good many of the boys to be found who had not a cent left of their two months pay. Every cent of it was gambled away. On the other hand there was some of the boys who had made *hundreds* of Dollars gambling. The orders are very strict against it, but that's all the good it does. If you should hear anything about persons belonging to the Co. sending more money home than some of the others do, you can *guess* how it is made. . . .

Well, we will get through with *this job* in a few days I hope, and thats going to *help* wind up the war, if it dont wind it up completely. We've got to *hurry* though if we intend to get in there by the 4th of July. That's the time set for us to get in. I guess we will have an easier time of it when Vicksburg is taken. There is considerable talk now about our Regt being detailed to guard prisoners *as soon as we take them.*

We had quite a brush with the rebels day before yesterday. I presume you will see the whole thing in the papers before you get this letter, but then I guess what little I say will not come amiss considering that I saw how the thing "was did." There is a large fort a little to the left of the front of our Brigade, and Gen Logan has been trying his best to take it ever since we came on the lines; for a few days past he has been undermining it, intending to blow it up. Well every thing was ready day before yesterday, and our Reg't was called out to man the rifle pits, so as to attract their attention in our front and prevent their reinforcing the men in the fort when Logan should blow it up and charge.

Well every thing was ready at three o'clock and the mine was fired. It did not do as much damage as was expected, but it startled them a little I can tell you. Just at that time one of Logans Brigades charged and went into the fort in less than no time, or rather into one end of it while the enemy held the other end. Logan's Pioneers then followed and threw up a breastwork to protect them, and they held the place until after dark last night when they were compelled to fall back in their old rifle pits again.

Our Regt was kept in the rifle pits until after dark when we were relieved and brought back to camp, but we have had to keep our guns stacked, and ourselves in readiness to fall out at any time either day or night. The Reg't was very lucky this time, we did not lose a man out of the Reg't in all the fight. The reason was that we were under cover all the time in the rifle pits. I have not heard what could be called anything like a correct estimate of our loss in the charge but it could not be very large.[4]

There was quite a little incident happened this fore-

---

[4] Logan's attempt to undermine the Confederate line is described by Andrew Hickenlooper, "The Vicksburg Mine," *Battles and Leaders*, III, 539–43. Logan was on the right center of the Union line. Grant estimated his loss at about 30 men killed and wounded. Grant (*ibid.*, III, 527–28) relates: "I remember one colored man, who had been under ground at work, when the explosion took place, who was thrown to our side. He was not much hurt, but was terribly frightened. Some one asked him how high he had gone up. 'Dunno, Massa, but t'ink 'bout t'ree mile,' was the reply."

noon. Dick Brighton was coming out of the rifle pits, where he had been sharpshooting all day, and one of the rebels fired at him; the ball struck just at his feet and he stooped down and picked it up, remarking at the time to one of the boys that the "Rebs" would regret throwing their shot around in that way. In the after noon he went back into the pits again and loaded his gun with the ball that he had picked up. He soon had a good chance to fire, and he did so with such good aim that the Secesh dropped, and Dick had the satisfaction of knowing that he had at least wounded a "Reb" with one of their own bullets. . . .

Love to all the family

Your affectionate Son James

H'd Q'rs 14 Wis Vols
In the Rear of Vicksburg
July 3/63

Dear Parents

It is nearly night and I have not much time to write but I guess I will have time to tell you the good news. Vicksburg is ours at last. *The 4th of July scared them so that they concluded it was best to give up,* and for my part I think it is the best thing they could have done. The boys here would not have objected if they had given up long ago.

I guess that we will not go into the city before tomorrow sometime. We will have our hands full for a few days now, I guess, taking care of prisoners, and I may not have time to write again for some time, but you must not worry on my account.

The boys are all in high spirits. Some of them can hardly

keep still, they feel so good over the surrender. My health is first rate. I have not time to write any more.

With love to all the family I remain

Your Affectionate Son

J. K. Newton

Head Q'rs 14th Wis Vols

Not in the REAR *of* VICKSBURG, *but in Vicksburg July 9/63*

My Dear Parents,

. . . When last I wrote you we were still outside of Vicksburg, but I dont know whether you rec'd the note or not. I was in considerable of a hurry, and could not write much; but tonight I have finished my work, and now I can write you a *long* letter, even if it is not very *interesting,* and first I must tell you how I spent the 4th.

In my opinion I had about as glorious a 4th of July as I could wish to spend. Early in the morning our Reg't was ordered to be in readiness to march at a minutes notice; we fell in, and stacked arms; all of us expecting to spend the day in Vicksburg, and—we were not disappointed. We "counted the minutes" until all was ready, when off we started. Our Reg't had the honor of leading the Brigade into the city. We all felt proud of it, I can tell you, for we had *worked,* and *fought* hard to obtain that privalege; and —"where there's a will there's a way" you know.

It looked strange to see Uncle Sam's troops marching through the city, and the Secesh standing in groups at every street corner, for you must know that they did not put the men under guard in the city: all the precaution that was taken to prevent their escape, was to place guards all round on their old breastworks to keep them somewhere within bounds until they could be paroled; but we need hardly to have taken that trouble, for the men here are only too glad to be paroled, and allowed to go home for a while.

They seem to have formed quite a good opinion of our men since we came in here. They did not expect to be treated so kindly and so respectfully, as they have been: and by treating them so we have quite won their esteem. A great many of them will not accept of any parole; but want instead to take the oath of allegiance and remain within our lines, or be sent north, they dont seem to care much which. Anyhow they say they have got "enough of fighting *us.*" . . .

There is a report in camp to night that our men have found 20,000 stand of new arms, that have never been used, but had been hid away by the Secesh, and no account was given of them by the Rebel General (Pemberton) when he surrendered to Grant. If such is the case Grant will undoubtedly send him north instead of "paroling" him as was intended.[5]

I went down to the old "Calaboose" where I was kept when I was in here before. It looked as natural as—*an old pig pen.* There was a grave in one corner of it, where I suppose some poor fellow was buried who died in there after I left. . . .

I presume there are a great many conflicting reports up north, as to what was gained on our side by the surrender of Vicksburg. I should not wonder if the Copperheads up there made it out to be not much of a victory after all, but notwithstanding what *they say,* and the stories that they circulate, the truth will come out in the end. As near as I

---

[5] The rumor was untrue. Confederate General John C. Pemberton was subsequently exchanged.

can find out our victory amounts to just this. We have now undisputed possession of the Miss: River. We have taken 31,000 prisoners; 45,000 stand of small arms; over 100 cannon; and nearly 100 stands of Colors. All this we have gained, besides the several thousand prisoners, and almost 100 pieces of cannon which we have taken in the several battles between Grand Gulf and this place. They are also fighting, with very good success to our arms, out beyond the Big Black. 600 prisoners have already been brought in and there are more coming: *reinforcements for the Doomed City,* we call them. There is no mistake about it, though, *they came rather late.*

I have sad news to write again, and I might as well tell it now as at any other time. Henry Cady is dead: he died on the 1st day of July, but we did not hear of it until yesterday. Capt Ward started at once for Millikens Bend to see what could be done for the rest of our boys there; that makes three of our Comp'y who have died in that hospital, and all for the want of proper care. None of them were so badly wounded but what they might have recovered if they had been sent north, or even cared for properly here; but no, they must be kept down here in this hot unhealthy climate until they either die, or are able to come back to the Reg't.

"Little Cady"—as we all called him, was universally acknowledged to be the best boy in the Comp'y; amid oaths and curses that would shock any one who heard it for the first time, he was never known to use an oath; he also kept free from all camp vices. There was not one in the Comp'y who would not do any thing for him. We all loved him dearly, and now he is taken from us. The boys all moarn for him, but myself especially, for he was like a brother to me, and I always considered him as such; he was always so good, kind, and accommodating, that every one who saw him took an interest in him at once. . . . I can but hope that he has gone to that better world where sin, pain, and sorrow can not enter. . . .

We are camped on a hill, just inside the Rebel works, about one mile from the city. We have the best camp ground now that we have had since we left Corinth—the boys say they had a better one, when at Grand Junction, but I wasn't there so I dont know. The duty here consists of picketing and fatigue; the pickets are placed on the Rebels line of old works all around the city. Our old entrenchments are being filled up as fast as possible. The duty is not very hard but it is constant; the men have to go on duty every other day regular. There is not much grumbling however for we all know this is a great deal better than carrying knapsacks and marching in this hot sun.

Really it is awful hot: in the middle of the day the sun actually scorches a person. There were several cases of sunstroke on the 4th, when we marched into the city; it was very hot and dusty to be sure, but it did not use me up as it did some of the boys. I dont know what the reason is but it is nevertheless true that since I got back to the Reg't I can stand twice as much marching and fatigue as I could before. . . .

I remain as ever

Your Affectionate Son

James

CHAPTER SIX

MISSISSIPPI
INTERLUDE

Head Quarters 14th Wis Vols
Natchez, Miss., July 18/63

My Dear Parents

It has been quite a long time since I wrote you a line but I have a very good excuse, as you will see by looking at the date of this letter. The fact is we have left Vicksburg, and come down the river to this place on a sort of foraging expedition. We left our tents & other traps in Vicksburg, together with the sick men belonging to the Co. I have heard however, lately, that they have all been sent for, and that we will spend the summer here.

It is a very pretty place, and I am sure I would like nothing better than to spend the summer in one place. I never did like moving, and now I hate it worse than ever. When we left Vicksburg we did not know where we were going, but we found out before we got here.

Our Reg't was detailed as Provost Guards. We have been

camped in the Court-house Square, while the other Reg'ts have had to do the foraging.

There is no end to the negroes in and around the city. Hundreds are flocking in every day. I expect we will get up a Reg't or two of Negroes before we leave.

I have some good news to tell you and I might as well tell it at once. I have got my Serg't warrent at last: the Capt was as good as his word, and promoted me to 2nd Serg't. . . . My pay after this will be $17 a month, not much of an increase, but then you know "every little helps." . . .

The general opinion, when we started, was that we would have a fight before we got back, and I am sure I dont know but what we will, too, for we were called up both last night, and the night before, and lay in line of battle from one o'clock, until daylight. The reason was that there was a small Cavalry force of some two or three hundred seen out here in the country a few days ago and there was no telling how many more there might be. We always intend to be ready for an emergency.

There was quite [a] little incident occurred here the other evening. A Negro woman came into the camp and told us there was a secesh soldier down town hid in his mothers house. He was on furlough and thought to escape some night and go back to the army. I went at once to the Col: and told him what I had heard, he gave me liberty to go down town along with a patrol and take him prisoner. The Negro women acted as guides and down we went, posted guards about the house, and then we went in and took the fellow; his mother was dreadfully frightened, but we soon quieted her fears, by promising that if he would allow us to parol him, he should return home that night. He was taken up to the court house, paroled, and set at liberty.

We are having very fine weather, and, I do not think, very hot, but the citizens here are all complaining of the heat. We have all kinds of fruit down here, Peaches, Pears, Apples, Figs, Melons, Green Corn, & all kinds of Vegetables. I have no time to write any more and my paper is gone so I will close by sending love to all the family.

Your affectionate son,

J. K. Newton
2nd Serg't—Co "F"
14th Wis Vols

Head Quarters 14th Wis Vols
Natchez, Miss. July 23/63

Dear Father & Mother:

I have been waiting very patiently for the mail to come expecting to get a letter, but when the mail came today I was disappointed for not a letter did I get, and now the only way I can console myself is to write one: that's one reason why I am writing now; another reason is, that I have a little time to myself just now, and I might as well improve it.

My health is as good as usual, for which I am very thankfull. Next month is the sickly month down here: whether there will be Yellow Fever here, or not: is not known; but some of the citizens here, think it highly probable, on account of our throwing up the earth, in building breastworks. They say that is never allowed to be done down here in hot weather on that very account. They all agree, however, that we are in as healthy a place as there is in the entire south. . . .

One of the Lieut's went up to Vicksburg yesterday to

get our tents, and the rest of our traps, so now, there is a great prospect of our staying here through the summer. . . .

The mortality is absolutely frightfull in Vicksburg among the prisoners and Negroes. Our men seem to stand it a great deal better than they do; probably because they are better clothed and fed. The number of deaths has been as high as one hundred in a day among the prisoners alone. That is the result of their being penned up in Vicksburg so long. I thought it would come sooner or later.

I declare, it is really too bad that I haven't had a chance to go out into the country. The boys who have been out bring back glowing accounts, but thats all the good it does. I cant enjoy it at all. Well, John Ryan [1] will be down here in a day or two, and then I wont have to act as orderly any longer, *or rather for a spell*. Wont I run around though, I rather think I will.

Well Capt Ward [2] has resigned and gone home. So now the "Institution" of Co "F" has got to be run by Depere men after this. I guess they are able to do it for to tell the truth they have been doing it this long time, only in his name: There's no mistake about it though the Co affairs are left in a better condition than they ever were before. Whether we will have another Capt of Co "F" I dont know. . . .

Will love to all the family I remain

Your Affectionate Son

James K. Newton

---

[1] Ryan had been home on leave.

[2] Delos A. Ward of Fond du Lac. Company F did without a captain until December of 1864, when Ryan was appointed. Meanwhile, Lieutenant Reuben Wheeler, of De Pere, commanded.

Head Quarters 14 Wis Vols
Natchez, Miss. Aug 3d 1863

My Dear Father & Mother

. . . I would have written a few lines and sent them by Dick Brighton but I had not time. . . . There was some little excitement too about that time, for we were expecting an attack on the city from the Rebel Col Logan,[3] who is out here in the country somewhere with a small force of Cavalry. He came within two miles of the city, and burnt two bridges. He did not dare to come any further however, and he was not allowed to stay there, for our mounted Infantry was sent after him in less than no time, and he concluded the best thing he could do was to leave.

He left—with our men in hot pursuit. He was followed until dark, when our men returned to camp, bringing with them about 30 prisoners. Among them were several paroled men who had their paroles with them; they will undoubtedly be hung, or shot. Logan has not been heard of since. I guess he knows better than to try to take this place. Anyway whether he does or not we feel perfectly safe.

For several days past we have been in the habit of sending out small squads of mounted Inf'y in charge of an officer to scour the country. One squad of five men with an officer went as far as the little Town of Fayette—about 30 miles from here: they made the citizens believe that there was a large force of *"The Yankees"* coming and that they had been sent ahead as a sort of scouting party; they gathered up 16 Rifles and shotguns, about 200 sheep, 60 head of Cattle, & 20 horses; they "pressed in" a horse and wagon to carry the guns, mounted a lot of niggers on the horses and made them drive the cattle and sheep, and then

---

[3] Probably Lieutenant-Colonel (afterwards Brigadier-General) Thomas M. Logan.

they left that neighborhood about as fast as possible. Considering the number of men, and the short time they were gone I think they did pretty well.

By the way though, I had almost forgotten half my story. When they got ready to leave they went to the hotel in the place and ordered supper for *40 men;* telling the Landlord to have it ready as soon as the main body came up and they had *posted the pickets.* The boys think they wouldn't like to go back after the supper without taking the 40 men with them. . . .

Give my love to all the family and remember me ever as

Your Affectionate Son

J. K. Newton

Head Quarters 14 Wis Vols
Natchez, Miss., Aug. 5/63

Dear Father & Mother;

. . . By all accounts there is considerable sickness in Vicksburg. It is an awful place truly. I am glad that we are not there; and I do hope that we wont have to go there again this summer.

Natchez is said to be the healthiest place on the Miss river south of the "Dixie line." For my part I think the reason is because it has been kept so clean. There are city laws here to the effect that no man can dig a cistern or disturb the surface of the earth in any way, within the limits of the city in the months of June, July, Aug & Sept. Also any person is liable to a heavy fine who allows any Vegetable, or animal matter to accumulate in, or about his premises. The "dirt carts" go over the city every morning & every thing is cleaned up.

I am sitting in the "Market House" (which joins the

Court yard). It is a long, open building—or I can describe it better by saying that there are four rows of pillars with a roof over them. It is about 150 feet long, by 80 feet broad. It is furnished with "stalls" and tables which are let to the different parties who have anything to sell. Beef is not allowed to be sold in any other place in the city. The meat is brought into the Market house in the evening and hung up to cool; about two o'clock in the morning the vegetables begin to come in, and the selling begins at the same time. From that time until 7 o'clock there is a perfect stream of people coming & going; and the house is crowded. It is a pleasant sight when seen for the first time, but it soon grows tiresome and we are camped so near that we get all the extra noise, which is considerable I can tell you. . . .

If the "copperheads" of the north only knew in what estimation they are held by the majority of the people of the south, I think they would shortly be disgusted with the cause they have espoused, and "wiggle" themselves out of sight—forever; which I prophesy they will wish they had done in a short time, for surely the war cant last much longer; with the news of such Victories as Vicksburg, Gettysburg, Port Hudson, Tullahoma, & Helena all coming in *one weeks* time. In my mind it will strike the death blow to Rebellion and I doubt not that the names of Grant, Meade, Banks, Rosecranz, and Prentiss [4] will be remembered and cheered, on each succeeding "4th" for years to come, for having added new glory and honor to that ever memorable day. . . .

---

[4] On or about July 4, 1863, General Grant forced Pemberton to surrender Vicksburg; General George G. Meade defeated Robert E. Lee at Gettysburg; General N. P. Banks captured Port Hudson, Louisiana; Rosecrans maneuvered General Braxton Bragg out of Tullahoma, Tennessee; and General Benjamin M. Prentiss defeated General Theophilus H. Holmes at Helena, Arkansas.

Our forces captured 150 bales of cotton a few miles from here and sent it in yesterday. There has been slight skirmishing for several days past. In a skirmish yesterday our loss amounted to one Lieut wounded, which is the first white man who has been wounded on our side since Logan's force came down in this part of the country. They have shot several Negroes. In fact they dont think anything of shooting *them* down. There is one nigger in town now who was shot 7 times by them more than a week ago, but he is alive yet. If it had been a white man he would have died long ago. . . .

Your Affectionate Son

James Newton

HeadQuarters 14 Wis Vols
Natchez Miss. Sept 6/63

Dear Father & Mother

. . . I have not written to you as often as I should have done if I had had more time, but I have been very busily engaged for the past two weeks. I was detailed, directly after John Ryan got back to the Camp, as Sergt of the Boat Patrol and I have been on Daily Duty ever since. The duty is not very hard but it is very rare that I can get more than half an hour to myself at a time. I have to station a guard at the Gang-plank of every boat as soon as it lands and examine all passes and search all baggage belonging to citizens before allowing them on board. Sometimes when there is a rush of boats it keeps us pretty busy. I believe though that it is all the better for me having some regular work to do. I am sure I like it better than I would any other way. The fact is we can be independent, and you will know that is something, when you have been obliged to run at the nod of one or two men as long as I have.

We have a nice little house down on the Levee where we sleep, and the neighbors were all so glad that there was going to be a permanent guard on the Levee that it seemed as if they could not do enough for us. They lent us a table, chairs, two matresses and then did not seem to think that we had ought to thank them, but rather that they were the obliged party. There is an old widow woman and her daughter who live right across the road. They cook our rations for us. We buy vegetables now and then and on the whole we manage to live pretty well. It really begins to seem like home. . . .

Your affectionate Son

J. K. Newton

Head Quarters 14th Wis. Vol. Infy
Natchez, Miss. Sept 14th 1863

My Dear Parents.

. . . When I wrote you last I was on duty at the Levee as Sergeant of the Boat Patrol, but now it is somewhat different. Our Reg't has been relieved from Provost Guard duty since then, & now I am on picket. I brought my knapsack along with me, because I expected the Reg't to move camp before I got back, so you see I had every thing ready to write, & I am sure I have time enough, & to spare.

I dont know exactly what we were relieved for; I have heard several reasons. One thing I do know, as soon as the Col. got back there was a fuss right off; he said at once that his Reg't should not stay in that place & be imposed on any longer & unless the Ass't Provost Marshall was re-

moved & a better man put in his place he would not stay another day. Accordingly the 72nd Ills went on Provost duty,
& our Reg't goes on Picket. We have about half the duty
to do now that we did before so you see we did not lose anything by the change. I believe I lost about as much as any
of them, for now I do not have my meals cooked up in style
as I have for the last month: well I have eaten "hard tack"
& bacon before, & I guess it wont hurt me now. This is the
first "Picketing" I have done since last spring when we
went up to American Bend on the cotton expedition.

This morning the Guirillas attacked the "Nigger Pickets" on the other side of the river & drove them in; not,
however, until they had quite a sharp little skirmish with
them. It was laughable, I can tell you, to stand on the bluff
and see the Niggers skedadling for their lives—as they
thought—to the bank of the river. There is a sandbar on
the other side, almost opposite the city, containing several
hundred acres; that was completely covered with them—
I suppose you know, there is a "corral" on the other side
containing several thousands of them. The "corral" was
deserted and its contents strewed along the river bank.

From where I stood I could see the skirmishing quite
plain; the Niggers behaved first rate. At the first intimation
of a row, one of the Gunboats anchored opposite; in a
good position to pitch the cast iron into the Secesh. I
wish that I could have stayed longer & watched the affair,
but just then I was called away to go on picket & had to
leave.

After I left, the 17th Wis, 95th & 11th Ills & 7th Kansas
were ferried across the river to participate in the row, &
there was a report came out to the picket lines that our
Reg't had been ordered to be ready to march with one day's
rations. I hardly believe it is true, though.

About a week ago the 4th Division of our Army Corps

went across the river & went out as far as Harrisonburg, on the Wachita I believe. The 17th Wis went with them & had quite a sharp little fight at Trinity. They burnt one steamboat belonging to the Rebels & took a fort built under the direction of Gen Beauregard [5] some time ago, and named after him; the 17th's loss was five men wounded, one mortally. It is getting so dark that I cant see the lines so I guess I will stop & finish this letter in the morning.

Good Night

Tuesday Morning Sept 15th 1863

Wouldn't I like to walk in & take breakfast with you this morning? I *guess I wont come though,* for I'd be sure to get into a row with Minnie [6] or Sarah, & that would spoil all, you know. How would you like to see me taking my solitary breakfast this morning—for I have not eaten it yet; but I will, as soon as one of the boys make some coffee. . . . My paper has "gin out" so I'll have to close. Love to all.

Your affectionate Son James K. Newton

HeadQuarters 14th Wis. Vo. Infantry
Natchez, Miss. Sept 24th 1863

Dear Father & Mother

. . . I dont want you to expect me home until you see me there, for it is very uncertain that I will get a furlough at all before my time is out. I expect as soon as another campaign is planned for this fall that furloughs will be "played out."

---

[5] General P. G. T. Beauregard.
[6] One of James's sisters.

Our Union Defenders.

Pittsburg June 2nd/62

Dear Parents;

It has not been many days since I wrote you quite a long letter, but I suppose you wont scold much if I dont wait for an answer to my last letter, as I have come to the conclusion that it wont hurt me to write every chance I can get. I am sure I dont know what I should do if I did not get a letter once in a while. I am afraid I would get homesick and that is the worst kind of sickness a person could have down here. I suppose before this time that Lieut Harrison has arrived at Depere, I would have written a letter and sent it by him if I had had time, I did not know that he was going until about half

Photograph of original letter. Courtesy of
State Historical Society of Wisconsin.

Union soldiers at Shiloh. From *Battles and
Leaders of the Civil War,* Vol. I, New York, 1887.

Hamburg Landing. Drawing by Alex Simplot. Courtesy
of John Hunter and State Historical Society of Wisconsin.

General Rosecrans and staff at Corinth. Drawing by Alex Simplot.
Courtesy of John Hunter and State Historical Society of Wisconsin.

Confederate attack at Corinth. Drawing by Alex Simplot.
Courtesy of John Hunter and State Historical Society of Wisconsin.

Siege of Vicksburg. From a painting by Chappel.
Courtesy of State Historical Society of Wisconsin.

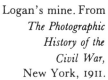

Logan's mine. From
*The Photographic
History of the
Civil War,*
New York, 1911.

The assault on Vicksburg. Courtesy of
the State Historical Society of Wisconsin.

Union works outside Vicksburg. From *Harper's Weekly*,
July 4, 1863. Courtesy of State Historical Society of Wisconsin.

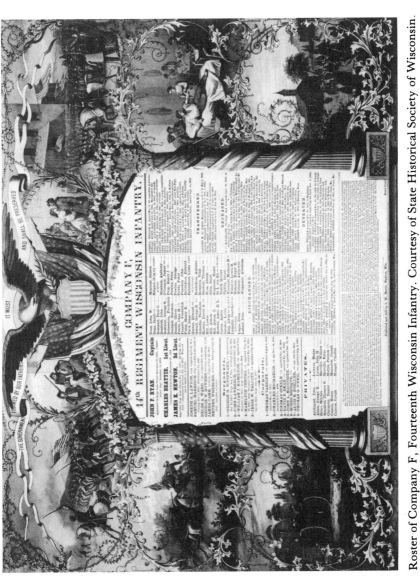

Roster of Company F, Fourteenth Wisconsin Infantry. Courtesy of State Historical Society of Wisconsin.

The expedition up the Red River. From
Battles and Leaders of the Civil War, Vol. 4, 1888.

The Battle of Nashville. From *Harper's Weekly,*
January 14, 1865. Courtesy of State Historical Society of Wisconsin.

James K. Newton at Oberlin College.
Courtesy of Oberlin College Archives.

James K. Newton.

Dont it seem strange that there should be so little sickness in New Orleans as there is this year. It looks providential and no mistake; for if it had been so sickly there this year as it is some years we would never have been able to occupy it through the summer.

The citizens here are waiting with great anxiety for Gen Grant to proclaim free trade on the river. I know a great many ladies in town who have not had a new dress of any description since the war broke out. The sutlers are not allowed to bring dry goods down the river. Sometimes there is one to be found who is more hardy than the rest & tries to smuggle some down the river but they dont make much in the end. They have their whole stock confiscated, themselves fined, & either have to leave the lines within a certain time or else they are imprisoned, so you see one man dont have a chance to try the game more than once.

I want you to tell Minnie that I am going to give her a lecture if she dont write pretty soon. I have been waiting an awful long time now, but I'll wait until the next mail, and then—look out. . . .

I believe I have told you all the news, if I haven't I will the next time I write.

Your Affectionate Son

James K. Newton

Head Quarters 14th Wis Vol Infantry
Vicksburg, Miss. Oct 18th 1863

Dear Mother:—

I rec'd your welcome letter dated Sept 24th more than a week ago. I hope you will consider my reason for not answering it before a good one when you stop to consider how much has had to be done within that week. I rec'd your letter at the same time we rec'd orders to pack up and get ready to march. We left Natchez & came up here to Vicksburg & have hardly got settled down in our new camp yet, but I thought it would hardly do to let it lay any longer for *"fear it might spoil,"* so I have set down at the present time to answer it. If I dont finish, it wont be my fault.

I guess I might as well tell the truth as not about my health; the fact is, I havent been as well as usual for ten days past. I have had one of my old headaches, and I guess about as hard an one as I ever had; however its all gone now & I am as well as ever.

You mentioned in your last letter of having rec'd that $30.00 that I sent you so long ago, more than two weeks before, and that you acknowledged its receipt in a letter written at the same time. Now I never rec'd that letter, & I have a suspicion that there has been several of your letters lost before reaching me. They must have been burnt on one of the many boats which have been destroyed on the river this summer.

It appears by the papers that the 1st Wis Cav was in the fight near Chattanooga.[7] I should think that Edward would surely write now if he is in the land of the living. I cant see what the reason is that he has not written to some one before this. Queer fellow isn't he. . . .

Some of the boys who were taken prisoners at the same time I was have just come back to the Regt lately. They stayed at Benton Barracks a while after I did, and then ran away & went home & have been there ever since until within a week or two, when they came back to the Reg't.

---

[7] The Battle of Chickamauga, Georgia, September 19–20, 1863. The First Wisconsin Cavalry was not engaged.

They all said that they were tired of staying at home was the reason they came back, not that they were afraid of being taken & brought back. . . . Not that I think the servise will be benefited very greatly by such men. They are just the ones who do the mischief and bring the servise into disrepute. I guess I've said enough . . . so I'll quit.

Love to all the family.

Your affectionate Son

James K. Newton

Head Quarters 14th Wis. Vol. Infy.

Vicksburg, Miss. Nov 7th 1863

Dear Father & Mother:—

. . . I believe when I wrote last I was not very well. I did have the Ague for several days, but I'm well as ever now. I got well just in time to make out the Pay Rolls; they aint quite done yet, but I will soon finish them. . . .

The Election day passed off in the pleasantest kind of a manner. Our Co polled twenty six votes for Lewis, but not one for Palmer, and that's the way the whole Reg't voted, not a single "Copperhead" in the Old 14th.[8] I think that's doing pretty well. There were 220 votes for Lewis in the Reg't. Some folks who did not know the size of the Reg't would think that number pretty small, but down here where we know the size of our Reg't, we are not surprised in the least that our Poll List was not larger. I was not quite old enough, as you know, to vote, or I would have

---

[8] James T. Lewis, Republican candidate for governor of Wisconsin, defeated Democrat Henry L. Palmer by a vote of 70,704 to 54,575. The soldiers voted 7,766 for Lewis, 542 for Palmer.

done what I could to make it larger. As it was I acted as Clerk of Election; About next spring, if the Copperheads need whipping at the Polls again I'll do what I can to help whip them. . . .

We were paid for two months a few days ago, and our Clothing accounts settled up for another year; there was about two dollars taken from my pay, as I had overdrawn my Clothing allowance on account of my having to draw so much in Benton Barracks last fall. You remember I had to lose all the Clothing I had at the time I was taken prisoner just because the Capt did not do as he ought to have done at the time I returned to the Reg't. I suppose I'm able to lose it so I aint going to bother myself about it. Give my respects to all inquiring friends. With love to all the family I remain

Your affectionate Son

James K. Newton

Head Quarters 14 Wis Vol Inf'y
Vicksburg Miss Nov 21/63

Dear Father & Mother:—
. . . The boys in the Co. are in good health and spirits. There is good prospect of our being paid soon, which maybe has something to do with it. . . .

Nov 22/63
I could not finish my letter so I will try & do so to-day. . . . This afternoon there is to be an inspection, and Brigade Dress Parade afterward. That's our way of spending the Sabbath.

When I got back from church this noon Lieut Wheeler

handed me a roll of bills which he said was *my share*. It
seems our Reg't was paid while I was down town, but the
Lieut drew my pay just the same. If the Paymaster was not
a very accommodating man he would not allow any such
thing. Lieut Wheeler is going to send some money home,
& I will send some in the same package. You may expect
$35.00 in the package. I wish I could double or treble the
sum, but I cant do it until they see fit to give me a commission.

By the way how would you like to have me take a commission in a "Nigger Reg't." I have been offered one once,
but I thought then that I could do better to refuse it & I
think about the same now, but I'd like to hear what you
would say on the subject.

They are getting out the Drums & I will have to close—
Do write as often as possible, for I never have any heart
to write unless I can get a letter sometime. Love to all

Your Affectionate Son

James K. Newton

Vicksburg, Miss, Dec 16/63
Head Quarters 14th Wis. Vols

My Dear Mother;—

I have not written to you for quite a long while, but it
was not my fault that I did not. While I was in the Hospital I did not feel much like writing I can tell you, and as
soon as I was able to leave there, I had all of a week's work
on hand waiting to be done. I went right to work at it, and
I have about finished it though not quite. Charley Ferris
is quite a good hand to write & he helped me a great deal,
or I would not have got so near through now.

I rec'd your letter dated Dec 6th this morning. I had been expecting one for more than a week, so you can imagine with what interest it was read. I am so glad to hear that you are getting along so well on the farm. I suppose you would not object much to my coming home again to go on and work with Samuel on the place. I am sure I would have no objections if the war was over. If I live long enough to see the end, I hope to come home, and see if I can not do a little better than I used to. I did not intend to enlist again until I had been discharged & been home for a little while; but I thought all the time, that if I got out all right this time I would eventually re-enlist. One week ago last Sunday the present excitement was started, and I re-enlisted with the rest of the boys. Whether you will like the idea or not I do not know, but I dont intend to write much more about it, but I will leave the subject to be discussed when I get home to spend the thirty days furlough which all the men are to have who re-enlist as Veteran Volunteers.

We expected to start for Wis. in time to spend New Years day, if not Christmas, at home but that idea is given up now, for Gen McPherson will not take the responsibility of letting us go upon himself, and there has been a dispatch sent to Gen Sherman (Commander of this dep't) at Chattanooga, stating the circumstances of our case, and as soon as an answer can be rec'd from him we will start for Wis. You may begin to expect us sometime about the 10th of Jan'y.

I guess it's about time I left off talking about that, and let you know something else which, maybe, will be as interesting. In the first place my health is getting to be first rate again, sometimes I can feel the same old chills coming on, but a good dose of Quinine is sure to break it up.

You say that I had better shake than take Quinine. Now

I beg leave to differ from you there, for I would take anything sooner than have the Ague all the time, even if I had to take Calomel itself. . . .

I have not half answered your letter but I must close for want of space. Love to all.

Yours &c J. K. Newton

Head Quarters 14th Wis Veteran Vol's
Vicksburg Miss Dec 25th 1863

Dear Mother:—

I rec'd your letter dated Dec 8th on the 20th. I had written a letter to you only two or three days before and I thought I would put off answering it for a few days. I did so, but I sat down the same day I rec'd your letter and wrote a long one to Edward. I thought if he was in the hospital he would *very likely* read it and probably answer it. I am glad to hear that he is getting better. It seems strange, does it not? that he should be so sickly down south here, when he was so strong and rugged while at home. I shall begin to think pretty soon that I can stand soldiering better than he can, notwithstanding you were so afraid when I first enlisted that I would soon fail. "I reckon"—as the saying is down here—that I have done Uncle Sam some good service since I enlisted, and I hope to do as much more at least, in the coming three years for which I have re-enlisted.

My health is first rate now. I am in hopes that I have got rid of the ague entirely but I carry Quinine with me all the time for there is no telling when it will come on.

You took quite a decided stand in regard to my accepting a commission in a Black Reg't. I dont know as I am in the least surprised. I asked you the question more to see what you would say than anything else. To tell the truth I did not feel hardly right about the matter, for I refused a commission as L't in a nigger Reg't when I knew all the time that if I accepted it, I could help you along a great deal more than I am now able to do, and I thought that if I could only get your opinion on the matter without your knowing anything about it, I would feel more satisfied. I have read your opinion of it, and you say that you speak Pa's sentiments too, and now we will let the matter rest. I am not so certain however that I would have refused it, had I been a private with no more interest in the Co than I had when I came back last winter. It would have been a little more tempting I think, but I always did say, and I say yet, that I would rather have the position I have now, than to be 1st L't in any nigger Reg't.

I guess I will have to drop the subject and close my letter too for it is getting quite late.

Your Affectionate Son

James

CHAPTER SEVEN

RETURN TO COMBAT

Cairo, Ill's, March 1st 1864

Dear Father & Mother:—

I have got so far on my journey, as you will see by the date of this: we left Milwaukee on Saturday, Feb. 27, morning, and arrived in Chicago about noon. From the cars we went directly over to what is called the "Soldiers Rest" (sometime I will describe it to you) where we found a nice dinner awaiting us. The news that we were coming had gone on ahead of us, and the Ladies had everything ready for our reception. We stayed there all night and on sunday morning at 9 oclock we started for Cairo on the Ills Central Railroad. And such a time as we had of it. It almost makes me sick again to think of it. We were crowded into some second class cars, and there we were for thirty-two hours. If I ever had the headache in my life I had it then. But its all over now and I'm glad of it too.

We arrived in Cairo yesterday afternoon at four oclock

and we were sent over to the Barracks (I dont know the name of them) and here we've been ever since, and I dont know how much longer we will stay, probably until there is a boat leaves for down the river.

There is a little snow here, about two inches I guess, and it is quite cold; there is a stove in each end of the Barracks, but it dont heat up much. The room is so open, my hands are so numb now that I can hardly hold the pen, so if you can only read what I write that is all I can expect.

Some of the boys think it comes harder to soldier it again after being home so long, but as for myself I knew just what was coming and prepared myself for it. It makes some of the new recruits wear pretty long faces I can tell you. I dont know as I can blame them for really it isn't pleasant. There is about 18 new recruits along with us and only about 22 of the Veterans. The rest were all left behind to be forwarded on as fast as they come in camp. When we all get together again, we will have quite a Reg't. . . .[1]

Its so cold that I cant write any more and for the same reason I cant write to Minnie though I would like to very much. I shall write again as soon as we get to Vicksburg. I will not have a chance before then but tell Minnie not to wait for me to write to her first, though I would if it was possible. Give my respects to all inquiring friends

Your Affec—— Son

James

---

[1] During the Civil War, Wisconsin was the only Union state that followed a policy of sending her recruits into old regiments instead of forming new ones. General Sherman said that he considered a Wisconsin regiment—because it was usually at full strength—equal to an ordinary brigade. The 14th Wisconsin, however, was soon split up and the two resulting "half" regiments were probably more nearly equal in size to those of other states.

Alexandria La
Wednesday March 23d 1864

My Dear Father & Mother:—

I did not think when I wrote you last, from Cairo, that such a length of time would elapse before I would be able to write again. And several other things have happened too, that I had no idea of at that time. In the first place I did not think that our Reg't would be started right off on such an expedition as this, without giving us time to get together even, much less to drill the recruits.

We reached Vicksburg on the 7th (March) & on the 9th we went on board the transport that brought us to this place. We left Vicksburg on the 10th and not until after we started did we find out where we were going. Up to the time of our getting on board the boat I supposed we were merely going on a foraging expedition, but when I saw the number of troops who were going I made up my mind that the foraging would be done on a grand scale. Undoubtedly you will hear all about it before you receive this letter; to tell the truth it will be a wonder if you receive it at all . . .

Our Reg't did not participate in the fight at Fort De Russa, although we would have done so had we been needed. We were about 1½ miles from the fort when the charge was made: "on the reserve" as they call it. Some other time I will tell you about the blowing up of the magazine at the fort. I have not time now.[2]

---

[2] General Andrew J. Smith took Fort de Russy (a few miles south of Alexandria on the Red River) from General Richard Taylor on March 12, 1864. Newton was a member of the Seventeenth Army Corps (General T. Kilby Smith), which, along with the Sixteenth Army Corps, had been detached from Sherman's Army of the Tennessee to support Banks in his Red River campaign. Admiral David D. Porter's fleet transported Newton and his fellow soldiers from

We have been here since last Friday doing nothing but move first on one side of the river and then on the other; it has rained most of the time. Today is the first pleasant day we have had. The new recruits think it rather hard to lay out in the rain night after night with only a blanket apiece; hardly any of them have a rubber; quite a number of them have been taken sick.

I have first rate health, *and no duty to do,* probably in consideration of how much I will have to do when we get back to Vicksburg. You cant imagine how nice it is to know that you wont have to go on picket as soon as it comes night, when marching along day after day: but then I know I'll have to make up for it when we do get back.

Gen Bank's advance joined us here a few days ago; they have had some skirmishing with the rebels, and have taken quite a number of prisoners. About 300 prisoners & 4 pieces of Artillery were sent in today. His dispatch says that he is driving the rebels and does not need any help. For my part I wish they would hurry up matters so as to get us back to Vicksburg where we can get a mail once in a while. I have not had a leter from any of you since I left Milwaukee, and it is almost 4 weeks since I left there. . . .

Give my love to all the family & dont expect me to write again until I get back to Vicksburg

Yours Affectionately

James

Vicksburg to Alexandria, Louisiana, where the force—under the general command of A. J. Smith—waited for Banks to arrive from New Orleans. When the two forces effected their combination, Banks set out for Shreveport, only to meet with disaster en route, at Mansfield. Meanwhile, Sherman had asked for the return of his troops, and A. J. Smith's force began a fighting retreat to Vicksburg. For an excellent account of the entire campaign, see Ludwell H. Johnson, *Red River Campaign: Politics and Cotton in the Civil War* (Baltimore, 1958).

Head Quarters 14 Wis Vols.
Vicksburg, Miss. May 24th/64

Dear Father & Mother:—

The famous "Red River Expedition" is over at last & we are out of Banks' Dep't. I hope we may never go near it again.

We arrived at this place this morning en route for—I dont know where. I have not time to give you a description of what I have been thro: I can only assure you that I am "all right" & that must suffice for the present. We hear that the rest of our Reg't is with McPherson on his campaign: we will probably join them as soon as possible.

We left the boat this morning, and are now camped temporarily near the City waiting for orders to proceed up the river. As soon as the boats have been cleaned we will go on board them again. I hope soon that we will have a resting spell, & then I can go on with the correspondence which has been interrupted for so long. Only think, I haven't rec'd but one letter from home, & that from Minnie, since I left home. The time has never seemed so long to me before.

I have written several times to you, and once to Minnie, but whether you have rec'd any of them, I can't tell. Some of them I know you have not for the Rebs took one of our transports that had the mail on it & we had the pleasure of picking up some of our own letters after the Secesh had read them.

As regards my health, I hope you may always enjoy as good as I have during the entire Campaign. I have been peculiarly blessed in that particular. Tell Minnie I will write to her as soon as possible, & to Mercena [3] also.

From all accounts the people of the north have been very

---

[3] One of James's married sisters.

anxious on our account. We have been in some pretty hard places but always managed to come out all right, especially our Reg't. Our loss was only five wounded during the entire expedition, none from our Co. You will hardly believe it when I tell you that we have been in six battles, besides being fired into times innumerable while on the Steamers. Only yesterday a single Guerilla fired three shots at our boat. They all fell short however. But I must close. Love to all.

Your Affectionate Son

James

I hope you wont forget to write soon & often.

Head Quarters 14th Wis Vols

Steamer J. S. Pringle, near Memphis, Tenn May 30/64

Dear Minnie:—

I answered your last letter once but, as I am certain you never rec'd my letter, I am going to answer it again. Doubtless you are entirely out of patience with me, and are ready to give me a regular scolding when you get a chance, but I hope you will forego that *pleasure.* . . .

Your letter dated March 6/64 came to hand April 27th and on the 28th—having the forenoon all to myself—I sat down and wrote you a long letter, and wrote one to somebody else. That very afternoon we were ordered out on a scout, and I had no opportunity to write again until I got back to Vicksburg, which was on the 24th of May: and then I only had time to write a short note, just to relieve the anxiety which I knew must be existing at home, but I knew you didn't care for short notes, any more than I do, so I put off writing to you until I could get a chance to write a passable sort of a letter. I dont know whether I shall succeed but I shall try to.

We started from Vicksburg on the morning of the 27th and now we are somewhere between Helena & Memphis. I think we will reach Memphis sometime this afternoon, when I expect to mail this letter and several others I have written, so that they will keep right on up the river with as little delay as possible. Where we are going is more than I can tell, but I expect we will join the rest of the Reg't, which is with McPherson in Georgia, where we will undoubtedly have some more active service to perform; that is, if they dont finish the campaign before we reach them.

When I left home I never suspected that within three months I could count the battles I have been in almost by the dozen, but such is the case. I was in three battles on the march from Natchitoches to Alexandria, one on the 22nd, another on the 23d and another on the 24th of April. I was in three others on the retreat from Alexandria to Morganza, one on the 6th of May about 14 miles from Alex., another on the 16th at Marksville, and another at Fort Morgan on the Yellow Bayou about three miles from Simsport on the Atchafalaya.

On the 6th while we were driving the rebels thro' a cornfield one of our boys picked up a piece of paper with some writting on it. As soon as we came to a halt he read it and passed it around for others to do the same. It was nothing "more nor less" than the following written by one of the Rebs.—the writing or spelling didn't give much credit to the writer.—Yanks: Magruder [4] of Texas will make you leave Alex. tomorrow morning, or you will have to fite like h———. We had supposed until then that Ma-

---

[4] General John B. Magruder.

gruder was at Galveston, Texas, but it seems that he had left that place and came up to reinforce Gen Dick Taylor —a degenerate Son of "Old Zack." [5]—*Notwithstanding the warning,* our forces did not leave Alex. until the Gunboats were all over the Shoals. . . .

Dont forget to write and write often. Tell me all the news

Your affectionate Brother

James

H'd Q'rs 14th Wis. Vol. Infy
Memphis Tenn June 4th 1864

My Dear Parents:—

. . . When I wrote last we were at Vicksburg. We got here on the 30th of May. We are camped about two miles from the city doing picket duty. The rest of the Brigade went out on a scout the day after we came here—after Forrest's band.[6] I think our Reg't was fortunate enough this time to be left behind, but we are paying for it by having to go on picket every other day.

I went out with the rest of the Co. day before yesterday —the first time I've been on picket for a "six months." The Co went out again today, but I did not go. Every other day on picket and doing other duty besides is more than I'm going *to volunteer* to do.

I have no idea what they intend to do with us. There is some talk of our staying here, and sending up for our

---

[5] Former President Zachary Taylor.
[6] General Nathan Bedford Forrest's cavalry.

things. They were at Cairo when we last heard from them. If they come down here to us, I guess the other part of the Reg't will join us too. I hope the Co. Books at least will be sent down, for the reports are accumulating fast and soon there will be a months work on hand for me to do. If the books were only here I could be at work on them now, but as they are not I'm doing nothing.

Serg't Lawrence joined us here. What a good time he must have had at home so long: and yet he didn't do right. I don't think I could have made myself contented at home so long, knowing that I had ought to be with the Reg't and especially if it was on such a campaign as we have been on for the last three months.

It was a pretty hard campaign, take it all around. But there's some consolation in knowing that it's over, and really on no consideration would I miss having been thro' the whole campaign. You can imagine though, how much better we would feel had it turned out as it had ought to —as Grant's campaign in Virginia is turning out, for instance. I suppose you get the news as soon as we do, so there's no use in telling you anything about that.

It has been raining here for the last two days, and, as we have no tents, we have been rather uncomfortable. I wish you could have seen us yesterday, our Rubber blankets spread over a couple of poles, and ourselves underneath them, enjoying the shower. In such a "fix" as that a person is bound to show out his real disposition. Some men were grumbling and growling all day long, others were laughing and joking and "carrying on" in every way imaginable to make fun, and keep up the spirits of the others. As a general rule you can expect more fun in camp on an unpleasant day than any other.

I have nothing to write about—so I may as well close,

hoping that when I do hear from you, you may be in as good health and spirits as

Your Affectionate Son

James

Head Quarters 14th Wis. Vol. Infy
Memphis Tenn. Wednesday June 22nd 1864

My Dear Parents:—

It has been more than two weeks since last I wrote you. I have been waiting all that time, and more too, for a letter from you; only think! I haven't rec'd a letter from you since I left home last winter.

Our Reg't is going to leave tomorrow with the rest of the expedition which has been fitting out at this place for the past two weeks, against Forrest: I hope we will be more fortunate than the other expedition was. You must have read all about it in the newspapers long ago, so I wont bother you with a history of it now.[7]

The rest of our Brigade started out this forenoon; we would have went with them if we had been paid, and as we had not, they left without us. We hope to get our money in the morning, and then go out on the cars, and join the Brigade. By so doing we will miss one days march at least. The Col. said that he would have the Express Agent come up here to camp for our accommodation. If he does not, it will be impossible to keep the men in camp, for they dont

---

[7] Newton is referring to Forrest's defeat of General Samuel D. Sturgis at Brice's Cross Roads, June 10, 1864. For an excellent account of "Old Bed," see Andrew Nelson Lytle, *Bedford Forrest and His Critter Company* (New York, 1931).

believe in carrying such an amount of money with them on a tramp, if they can help it.

If I get paid I shall send Eighty five ($85.00) dollars home. You will take ten dollars of it to make up for that ten dollars I borrowed of you last winter. Twenty five dollars you will use for the benefit of Mercena, as you see fit. The remaining Fifty dollars you will keep subject to my order. If we are paid again, before, or soon after, joining the other part of the Regt I shall not want to use it: and if you should want money, use it, of course.

I suppose you understand that if *things turn out as I have every reason to expect they will*, I will need *an outfit*, and it will take money to buy it too. But everything is at a standstill now, and will be until we join the other part of our Reg't. . . .

I have had the Ague again, as you said I would but I didn't have it in the spring. On the contrary it was near the middle of June. It was brought on by my standing for several hours in the hot sun on the 10th inst.

There were three men shot that day for committing an outrage upon the person of a defensless female who lived a short distance from this place. All the troops here not on duty were ordered out to witness the execution. Our Reg't went out at One o'cl'k and we had to stand there till after four, before the execution was over. The "shooting party" consisted of thirty six men & three Serg'ts from the 8th Iowa Infy—twelve men and a Serg't for each man, with one half of the guns loaded with blank cartridge. This is the first execution that has taken place in this Dep't that I know of, but I'm afraid it wont be the last. . . .

We have had rather queer weather down here this summer. While we were up Red river it didn't rain any to speak of for nearly two months, but since we came to Memphis it has rained almost every other day. It is raining now, and I assure you it isn't very pleasant writing under a Rubber blanket with the rain spattering on the paper every little while. I hope you'll be able to read this, but I cant tell, I'm sure.

Give my love to all the family,

Your Affectionate Son

James

Memphis, Tenn July 25/64

Dear Father & Mother.

. . . I have been down with the ague again, that was the reason I have not written to you before. I knew that you would hear from other sources, that I had escaped as usual without a wound in our last battle and so I knew you wouldn't worry about me. Tomorrow is my sick day, but if the ague dont happen to come on I will have my hands full of writing for the Co. I'm sure I dont know when I shall be able to give you an account of the expedition. I guess I'll have to put that off till I go home, as I have a great many other things.

Home! how sweet the word sounds. I'm sure I'll know how to appreciate a good home, if I'm allowed to return to it when peace once more reigns thro' the land.

Our Reg't was so fortunate as to capture a Secesh flag. We have had crowds of visitors since we returned just on that account. I really believe we're getting to be—notorious.

The Expedition was entirely successful, having accomplished fully what it was intended to, but you will read all about it in the papers, so I will say no more about it. Our Co. was very fortunate I think in having only one man wounded, considering the severe fire we were obliged to undergo. Chas Michaelis is the man who was wounded, he lives somewhere over in Lawrence. A Minnie ball passed thro' his right fore arm, but without breaking the bone. Lieut Wheeler, Hamilton Thetro, & Joe Laundry were each hit by spent balls, but not hurt. . . .

I shall write again as soon as possible, & I hope you wont forget to write once in a while to Your Affectionate Son

James

H'd Q'rs 14th Wis Vol Infy
St. Charles, Ark. Wednesday Aug 10/64

My Dear Father & Mother:

. . . You will see by the date of this that we have changed our H'd Q'rs since I wrote last; we came to this place quite unexpectedly, last Saturday (Aug. 6). We left Memphis on the 3d to the great grief of our "hundred day friends," [8] who could not see how we could appear so cheerful when we were going off no one knew where. It's got to be an old thing with us now, so we dont mind it, & their lamentations were entirely lost.

You may not know where St. Charles is situated so I will tell you. It is a small town—or rather a good site for a town —on the west bank of the White river, about 20 miles from Duvals Bluff, which is the base of supplies for Steele's army at present. There is a railroad from the latter place to Little Rock.

There are three other Reg'ts here besides ours, & we're

---

[8] Men who were allowed to enlist for a one-hundred-day period.

placed here to hold this position.[9] It isn't very well fortified yet, but it soon will be, for there are heavy details at
work on the breastworks every day, & with doing other
fatigue duty, as well as picket, the men are kept very busy.
As I am Co. Cl'k I escape all that, but I'm kept pretty busy
writing in the daytime. I have the nights to myself. . . .

One of the boys discovered a smoke down the river about
half an hour ago & the whole Regt has been watching it
ever since, hoping it will prove to be a mail boat. It has
just come round the bend, & proves to be a Steamer with
a couple of barges in tow, now for a mail. This is the first
boat that has come up the river since we came up. I'm
sure there must be letters for me, & I hope *one* from you,
at least. What a long—long time it's been since I rec'd
your last letter. . . .

Thomas Stewart has been reduced to the ranks at last.
I've expected it for a great while. The reason was "Coward-
ice before the enemy." In our last battles out near Tupelo,
he left the Co. every time & was not to be found till after
the fighting was over. When we got back to Memphis an
order was read to the Reg't reducing him to the ranks. If
it had been my case I think I would rather have been *under
ground,* than to have been branded as a coward before the
whole Reg't. . . .

The mail has come, & no letter from you, so I will not
have to answer any. . . .

The news is not quite so cheering as we hoped, but we'll
hope for the best no matter how dark things look. We have

---

[9] Newton was part of A. J. Smith's force (4,500 strong) passing up
the Mississippi River to join Sherman's army in Georgia. General
Rosecrans, however, needed the troops to check Confederate Sterling
Price's advance west of the Mississippi, so the men went to Arkansas
instead of Georgia. For an account of the subsequent campaign, see
Wiley Britton, "Resumé of Military Operations in Missouri and
Arkansas, 1864–1865," *Battles and Leaders,* IV, 374–77.

not heard from the other part of the Reg't for some time, but I can not think that they have gone thro' all those heavy battles near Atlanta without having some loss: according to the papers the heaviest part of the fighting was done by the 17th Army Corps.

I have not had the ague for some time now, & I hope I've broken it up. When I do not have "the shakes" I feel first rate—can eat my rations as well as the next one. Every time our bread gives out, Ryan & I have a long talk about *those men who cut down our rations,* & wish that they were situated so that we could cut down theirs. I dont think they would want them cut down more than once. When Ryan has a better appetite than usual, I have to remind him of the fact, by "hoping that he'll have the ague soon." By the way, my appetite is pretty good now, I guess, for he has wished several times lately "that he could catch me shaking." You see we have the ague by turns. When Ryan's sick I eat all the rations, & when I'm sick, Ryan eats them. But sometimes, you see, we feel pretty well at the same times & then the *rations cant hold out any how* we can fix it. . . .

With love to all the family, I am

Your Affectionate Son

James

H'd Q'rs 14th Wis Vol Infy
St. Charles, Ark. Sunday. Aug 21/64

Dear Father & Mother:

I can find no better way of spending a part of the Sabbath than by writing. Since we came here we have had no chance to go to church, as we had at Memphis, and our Sabbaths have been spent in camp in reading, writing— and by some in playing cards & such like. . . .

I have been engaged for a few days past in building an oven for the Co. I had a couple of men to help me, & of course I wasn't expected to work much, only to do the *engineering,* but I made up my mind from the way the men worked that we wouldn't get thru in a week, & so I had one man to bring mud, & another brick, & I did the bricklaying myself. The result is that the oven is up, we finished it after dark last night. The Col came over this morning to look at it & pronounced it a good job—you know he'd ought to know for he's the *rankin'est* man in the Reg't. I expect to have all the ovens to build after this. *Maybe I'll be brevetted Lieut. or something of that kind for "rendering such effective service to the country."* . . .

With love to all the family & respects to everybody in general, not tainted with Copperheadism, I remain

Yours, &c.

Jas. K. Newton

H'd Q'rs 14th Wis. Vol. Infy
Brownsville Station, Ark. Sept 9th 1864

My Dear Mother:—

Your welcome letter dated Aug 6th was rec'd on the 31st, more than a week ago. Had it been possible I would have answered it at once, but we were under orders to march when it was rec'd, & we have been on the move ever since.

We were paid off on the 31st for two months. Didn't get any Bounty [10] this time although the 3d installment was

---

[10] When Newton re-enlisted he received a bounty, probably amounting to about $300.

due. The Paymaster didn't have money enough with him to pay it. It will come just as good next payday. We left St Charles on the 1st and reached Duval's Bluff in the forenoon of the next day. Lieut Wheeler found an Express office there & I had him express $25.00 to you, which I hope you have rec'd by this time. . . .

We went on board the boat again on morning of the 3d & started up the river (White river) on a sort of an expedition. At that time I didn't know anything about what we were intended to accomplish up there, but I have found out since. Our orders were to proceed up the river to Augusta & rout—if possible, any force which might be at that place.

Augusta is something over one hundred miles from Duval's Bluff. We were not interrupted in our passage up the river until the afternoon of the 4th when we were fired on from the bank, by a force of Rebs who lay behind the Levee so that we had no chance at them. We effected a landing however, & drove them off in double quick time. An old citizen who was taken & brought on board the boat, said they passed his house on the gallop shortly after we landed, in force about four hundred. Our loss was three killed & about fifteen wounded. The Col. commanding the expedition was wounded, & Col. Ward, of our Reg't being the next in rank, took command.

The next day we went on up the river & captured Augusta without resistance, the Rebel force there having left on hearing of our approach. As we had accomplished the object of the expedition, we started down the river again & reached "The Bluff" in the afternoon of the 6th inst. Stayed there over night & then went on board the cars & came out to this place. . . .

What is Sam'l doing now. I suppose he had to take his chance with the rest in the draft that has lately come off. We are all anxious to hear how it has turned out. I hope

you wont forget to write all about it, & let me know all the news too. . . .
Love to all

Your Ever Affectionate Son

Jas. K. Newton

H'd Q'rs 14th Wis. Vol Inf'y
Brownsville Sta Ark Sept 17th 1864

My Dear Mother:—

I have two letters to answer, from you, an event which has not taken place before in an age. I wrote you about a week ago, & a day or two after I recd your letter dated Aug 29th, informing me of Samuel's enlisting.[11] I thought I would wait a day or two before answering it, as I had written you such a short time previously, but the next day we rec'd marching orders; we packed up everything, & got ready to start, but they were not ready for us then, and as there was no telling how long we would be gone when we once got started, Lieut Wheeler wanted the payrolls made out before we went, so I went to work on them. I completed them last night after dark, & just about the same time I rec'd your letter dated Sept. 4th. We are under marching orders yet but there is no telling when we will start.

I'm afraid we'll be gone long enough this time, we generally are when it takes so long to get started. No one has any idea where we are going, & I'm afraid we wont get letters, or be able to write any till we get back.

---

[11] Samuel had enlisted in the First Wisconsin Cavalry on August 27, 1864.

It's too bad Samuel had to enlist, but I'm sure you would rather have him enlist than be drafted. Do you remember what Pa said when I first spoke to him about enlisting? that "when I was drafted he would consent to my going and not before." I wonder what he thinks about it now.

The marching orders have come at last. We are to move at one o'cl'k. Its now almost noon, so I must hurry up. . . .

With love to all I remain
Your Affectionate Son

James

Cape Girardeau Mo.
Oct 6th 1864

My Dear Father & Mother
& all the rest of the loved ones at home:—

I wish I had that letter that I finished up in such a hurry there at Brownsville, now, I would see if I couldn't finish it up in a different style. I haven't any more time now than I had then but I have the advantage now of knowing just how much time I can spend in writing to you, while then, I thought I would have "lots" of time &—didn't.

We reached this place last night and today I have been eating & working alternately. You cant imagine how good it seems to have a plenty to eat after going on short rations for so long a time. We expect to leave here soon for St. Louis or Memphis, maybe tomorrow. I have been as busy as could be all day making out the Co. reports. We have been gone so long that we have got behind hand again, & all these reports have to be made out as soon as possible.

I have had better health on this march than ever before.

The only thing I had to complain of, was the want of shoes. My boots were worn so completely out, when we had still one hundred miles to go, that I was afraid I would never be able to travel the balance of the way, but I managed to ride a part of the last two days, & now I'm all right for another march of the same kind if they'll only give me a pair of shoes.

We traveled 290 miles in all—the longest march that I was ever on. But I wont say anything about it now for I haven't time, but some time I'll write about it if I have time while the events are fresh in my memory. . . .

Yours Affectionately

Jas. K. Newton

Glorious news from Virginia & Georgia, isn't there. I was certain there would be if we were gone long enough, but I didn't expect to be gone till this time.

H'd Q'rs 14th Wis Vol Infy
In the field after Price, Mo. Oct 21st/64

Dear Father & Mother:—

I have "taken time by the forelock," & now I'm going to write you a few lines, but I dont know whether you will ever get them or not. For some reason or other we do not get any mail ourselves nowadays, & I dont know whether our letters will go all right or not. . . .

We left "the Cape" on the 7th—the next day after I wrote you last—& went to St. Louis by Steamer. The Reg't didn't leave the boat when we reached that place, for we stayed only long enough to draw Clothing from the Post

Q'r Master, and then we started on up the river for Jeferson City. . . .

Reached Jefferson City on the 15th, & as soon as we could load our baggage on the cars we came out here—we are about 50 miles from Jeff. City & camped on the Le Meine river. The town of Ottersville is about one mile further on. The bridge across the river was burnt by some of Price's men when they went thro' here, & our Brig. is here to unload the cars on this side of the river, & load them on the other. The supplies for the whole army are in that way taken to Sedalia—the end of the railroad. There are a lot of men at work on the bridge now, so there is some prospect that we will not have this work to do *always.*

There are reports circulating thro' the camp that Gen. Blunt was beaten yesterday, & that Price now had a road clear for his retreat, but the report is by no means to be relied on. Our last reliable news was that Gen's. Curtis & Blunt [12] were on the other side of Price, while Gen. Smith was after him on this side & a force of Cavalry—about 12,000, were to the South of him. When last heard from— day before yesterday—Price's H'd Q'rs were at Lexington. There is every reason to hope that Price will lose his whole train, if not his whole army, before he gets out of Mo. . . . Gen. Rosecranz says we will go to Atlanta as soon as this expedition is over. We have been sent for several times but we were always situated so that we could not be sent just at that time. Its too bad too, for the boys in the detachment can not get any pay until we get together. Most of them

---

[12] Major-General James G. Blunt was in command of the District of South Kansas at this time; Major-General Samuel R. Curtis, of the Department of Kansas.

have been without pay for a year, & I suppose they dont feel very well in consequence. . . .

Don't forget to write all the news when you do write. By the way, aint it awful cold weather just now. We had a "young snowstorm" here yesterday, & it's been awful cold ever since we came to Cape Girardeau. But I must close.

Love to all,—that is, most every one,

Your's Affectionately

Jas. K. Newton

H'd Q'rs 14th Wis Vol Infy
Warrensburg Mo. Oct 27th/64

My Dear Mother:

. . . We have made another move since I wrote last, & had a pretty hard time generally, but I hope that it wont last long now. We left our camp the day after I wrote you; having rec'd marching orders about dark—to march in one hour—we pulled up stakes & left for Sedalia; reached that place about one o'cl'k & camped on the open prairie. The wind blew a perfect hurricane all night, & we were most froze before morning. I hugged up to a barn as well as I could, but the cold would get hold of me, & by morning I was ready to—take a good cup of coffee, I assure you.

We got thawed out about ten o'cl'k & started on; marched 18 miles, & camped in a better place than we had the last night; it wasn't quite as cold either, but the water froze so that I saw ice more than an inch thick the next morning. Started about daylight the next morning & reached this place about one o'cl'k; went into camp on a hill near the town where we've been ever since.

What nice times I've had trying to write, I'll leave you to

imagine. It has been very cold with a high wind every day. Today I made a table in the Quartermasters tent, to write on, & I assure you I've made it pay for what it cost to build it.

I hope we wont have to stay up here in this cold country long; there's some prospect of the Reg't's getting together as soon as this campaign is over. There has been a series of fights out here with Price & on the whole he got the worst of it, but why he was not used up entirely is more than I can see. He has been compelled to burn a portion of his Train, but will get off with a good Share of it. I have no doubt that the Cav. will follow him as long as he is in Mo. & then very likely he will run against Steele when he gets down in Ark. I believe in hoping for the best always, but I cant but think that someone is at fault for letting him get away from us. All thro' the campaign it has seemed to me as tho' there was "a screw loose somewhere," "Old Roza" [13] is at the bottom of it, I'm certain.

It's getting so cold that I'll have to stop for tonight. Maybe I'll write a little more in this before I mail it if I have time, but for the present Good night,

James

Oct 28th Morning—
I must tell you the news before I mail this. There's been a "big fight" out here somewhere near Independence & Price has been badly whipped. Marmaduke was taken prisoner & 2000 men; one General & I dont know how many men killed; 100 wagons taken, & the whole of his ammunition Train blown up; all of his Artillery was taken but one piece; & how he is going to get out of our way now, is more

---

[13] Rosecrans.

than I can see. A number of wagons loaded with "hard tack" have just been sent out to meet our victorious, but slightly hungry army.[14]

I hope that when I write again it will be from some other place a little further south; for I didn't enlist to soldier so far north as this. . . .

I must close for good now for it wont do for me to let the work go any longer, and there's "lots to do."

Love to all the family

Your Affectionate Son

Jas. K. Newton

H'd Q'rs 14th Wis. Vol. Infy

St'r Gen. Grant, on Mo. river near Herman, Mo.

Wednesday Nov. 9th 1864

My Dear Mother:—

I rec'd your very welcome letter of Oct 23d yesterday morning. The reg't rec'd marching orders and left Warrensburg on the 7th. We reached Jeff. City that night & the most of the Reg't stayed on the cars till morning, but Ryan & myself went up to the Capitol, & slept on the rotunda. We had a good *solid* bed & no mistake, but the stone pavement was pretty cold.

The next morning the Reg't left the cars & were taken up to the Capitol & stacked inside in one of the halls, & 'twas well we got up there in time, for in a short time the rain began to pour down, as it knows how to only in this

---

[14] This battle, at which Confederate General John S. Marmaduke was captured, took place in Linn County, Kansas, near Mine Creek, a few miles south of the Marais des Cygnes River.

southern country. If it had not been that we had such momentous business on hand I'm afraid we would have had to "stand the storm" no matter how long it was going to last.

The business which I allude to you will readily guess was hold the Election. Our greatest trouble was the want of tickets, but we managed to get hold of some which were intended for another district & altered them so that we made them answer our purpose. Lieut Wheeler, Ryan & myself acted as Inspectors of Election for our Co. & I cast the first vote I have *ever* cast, for the Election of Lincoln & Johnson. In doing so I felt that I was doing my country as much service as I have ever done on the field of battle.

There were 22 votes polled in our Co. & *not a Copperhead among them.* Owing to the want of tickets we could not vote for county officers; we did not know who to vote for, or the tickets might have been written, but I guess it dont make much difference either way. The thought would arise tho' that the Union Candidates must be very certain of carrying the day in Brown Co. or they would not run the risk of losing so many votes.

There were 172 votes cast in the Reg't: 140 for Lincoln, & 32 for McClellan.[15] If it had not been for the men who used to belong to the 17th being in our Reg't, we would hardly have heard from "Little Mac" at all.

After the election was over we went, or rather *came* on board the St'r Gen. Grant, & at daylight this morning started down the river; the wind was rather high when we started & about noon it had increased to such an extent that the boat was obliged to tie up to the bank; the wind is very cold & were we on the hurricane deck, I dont know

---

[15] General George B. McClellan, Democratic candidate for President.

what the boys would do. As it is the Reg't are all congregated in the Engine room where they are kicking & jumping around, making all the noise imaginable. I am seated in the cabin, where I have a first-rate chance to write, *considering*.

I'm glad to hear that you're getting along so well at home, but really it's too bad that we should *all* have to be away from home when one, at least, is needed so much. I dont like the idea of those *little girls,* Sarah & Marion's having to do so much that the boys had ought to do; but I cant prevent it; I'm sure I wish I could.

I hope that shortly after the results of the Presidential Campaign become known we will be no longer needed & then will start for "home again." I'll give it as my private opinion that the Presidential Campaign will in the end prove itself to have been the most effectual campaign of the war. What I have always thought, was, that all that was needed was to give the Copperheads of the north a whipping so that they would stay whipped, & soon after, we would have peace, & a much more effectual & better peace than they could have negociated, even tho' they had "exhausted all the resources of Statesmanship." Well: all I can say on the matter wont have the least effect now; but in a few days we will know whether we, constituting as we do the war power of the Union, will be upheld by the masses of the people in the north, or whether we have got to work out our own salvation; for if such an event should befall us—tho' I dont think it at all probable—as the election of McClellan, you will hear of some great doings between now & the 4th of next March: & the Rebels too, will both hear & feel, to their sorrow. . . .

My paper is full so I must close. Love to all the "little girls" & some of the big ones too from

James

[telegram] St. Louis, Mo., Nov 17th, 1864

Dear Father & Mother.

I've managed to get hold of a "7,30" Bond for 100 Dolls which I wish you would keep safe for me; [16] when the Coupons become due I think you can get the cash for them at Green Bay; if not, they are good any time. My health is first rate; I only hope yours is as good. I haven't time to write more as I'm in the Express Office among the crowd. Love to all.

Yours &c

J. K. Newton

---

[16] A thirty-year bond bearing 7 per cent interest.

CHAPTER EIGHT

ROUTING
THE CONFEDERACY

H'd Q'rs 14th Wis. Vol. Infy
Nashville, Tenn. Dec. 2d 1864

Dear Father & Mother:

I have to improve all the small pieces *of candle* I get
hold of to write by for lately I'm so busy during the day
that I dont have any time to myself. I am enjoying first
rate health at present, in fact my health could not have
been any better than it has been for some weeks. I have a
appetite that would scare you if you could see me eat once,
& you'd begin to wonder how Uncle Sam manages to feed
so many men with such appetites. The Ague has not
troubled me since I was at Brownsville, Ark., & I'm pretty
certain that at last I've got entirely rid of it.

As you will see by the date of this we have changed our
comfortable quarters at Benton B'ks & gone into the field

again; we've got to the detachment at last. They wouldn't
come to us so we had to come to them. We have a large
Co. now, more than sixty men present. . . .

We are having great times here at present. I dont know
but that the "Rebs" intend to make us fight if we hold
this place; there's one thing tho' if they intend to drive us
out they have got a big job on their hands, bigger than they
bargained for by a great deal.

Hood's Army is now about 18 miles from here; they had
a big fight out there day before yesterday, & today the
cannonading has been very heavy. What the result is I
know not, but without doubt we have been successful as
usual or we would not be laying here.[1] Day before yesterday we took 1200 prisoners & one General, not very bad,
is it?

Altho' there is not much danger of the enemy's getting
so far as this, still the troops are engaged fortifying. We are
at present camped in line of battle about two & a half
miles from the City. The whole Reg't is on duty tonight,
part of them digging—throwing up fortifications—& the
rest guarding them while they work. As I am Co. Cl'k I
escape all such unpleasant jobs, but then I have enough
else to do.

I suppose Sam must be somewhere about here, but I can
hear nothing of the Reg't & in fact I dont know whether
he is with the Reg't or not. I dont see why he dont write
to me; if I knew where he was I'd manage to drop him a
line & bring him to his senses. . . .

I must close. Dont forget to write often & tell me all the
news. . . . I hope you didn't forget to eat a thanksgiving
dinner for me. My dinner that day was *rather plain* but I

---

[1] Confederate General John B. Hood's forces were badly defeated
at the battle of Franklin, Tennessee, on November 30, 1864.

trust that didn't prevent my being thankful for my other blessings.
Love to all the family,

                              Your dutiful Son

                              Jas. K. Newton

                              Nashville, Tenn.
                              December 10th, 1864

My Dear Mother:
    I rec'd your kind letter of Nov 26th Several days ago, but until now I have had no opportunity of answering it. I'm afraid I wont be able to write long now before I'll get froze out & have to stop. We have had some awful cold weather lately, & it stormed for two days. The ground is now covered with ice to the depth of two inches which makes it anything but pleasant for us "boys" who dont carry around houses to live in, but notwithstanding the exposure I have first rate health, probably because I try to take as good care of it as possible.
    You say that Samuel is somewhere about this place. I wish I could see him, but I might as well hunt for a "needle in a haystack" as to hunt for him, & besides we are not allowed to run about any lately since Hood has been menaceing Nashville. I can not find out anything about the 1st Cav.[2] as yet. I dont know where they are, but if they're any where about here they must be across the river.
    I hope to run across him as soon as we have whipped out Hood, which will be very quick, I hope, for I dont care about laying behind these breastworks much longer.

----

[2] The first Wisconsin Cavalry, Samuel's regiment.

We had orders this evening to be ready to march at a moments notice, but we have had such orders so often lately that I dont know whether these will amount to anything or not.

There has been no fighting of any consequence about here since the battle of Franklin: the Rebs were signally defeated in that battle, their loss was over 5000 while ours was only about 5 or 600, quite a difference I think. I dont believe Gen Thomas [3] means to let Old Hood get off without any other battle & there is no telling when that will come off.

I hope you will always write good long letters like the last one, for I do love to get long letters. I would write a longer letter this time if it was not so cold but my fingers are so stiff now that I cant move them, thats the reason I am writing such a "loud hand." Love to all & tell Ed to write to me

Your dutiful Son

James

After Hood. Tenn
Dec 24/64

Dear Father & Mother:

The battle is over & I'm all right, in good health & spirits. The others are all right also

Yours in haste

James

---

[3] Brigadier-General George H. Thomas (promoted to major general on December 15), in command of the Army and Department of the Cumberland.

From Samuel Newton, James's brother.

Bowling Green.
Sun. Jan. 1st 1865

Dear Brother & Parents

You see by the date of this that I have changed my place of residence. We left Louisville on the 4th (of December) and went to Franklin and then turned off after Lyons.[4] We overtook them at Hopkinsville had quite a little brush with him. I was out on the skirmish line and the way the balls whistled around my head was not slow. We followed them up to Elisebathtown, took a few prisoners and one piece of cannon, that is all that it has amounted to. The rebels done considerable damage to the railroad and public buildings in every town.

I spoke to Capt Shepman about your discharge and he called the Lieut right in and told him what to do. He said that you had ought to have it and he would do the best he could but he was afraid there would be one difficulty and that was that the Mustering officer had committed suicide and he was afraid that all the blanks that were signed by him had been used. If they were he said that it would be quite a while before he could get it for you.[5]

I believe now that we are on our way to Nashville, we arrived here yesterday and leave tomorrow. I should have written yesterday but the weather is so cold that it took us all day to keep from freezing to death through the night

---

[4] Confederate General Hylan B. Lyon.

[5] Edward, who was sick during most of his stay in the army, was mustered out on October 31, 1864. "Captain Shepman" was Stephen V. Shipman of Madison.

for it is most awfull cold at present. A great many of the boys froze their hands & feet so as to lay them up some time. I had the diarrhea so that it came very near laying me up but I think that I will weather it out yet. The old boys say that they never suffered so much from hard [cold?] as we did while we were after Lyons.

Well I will close for I dont feel in writing mood and the smoke is almost blinding my eyes. With love to all the family I remain your

affectionate brother

Samuel

H'd Q'rs 14th Wis. Vols.
Near Clifton, Tenn. Jan'y 3/65

Dear Father & Mother:

We've reached the Tenn. river at last—had a pretty hard time taking everything into consideration, but notwithstanding all the fatigue & exposure we have passed thro' my health is, as usual, firstrate.

I rec'd a letter from you several days ago while we were on the march, but I've no time to answer it now. As soon as possible I'll write you a good long letter. As it is I can only assure you of my continued good health & also that you & all the rest of the family are remembered with much love by

Your Affectionate Son

J. K. Newton

P.S. John Ryan has rec'd his commission as Capt of the Co. & *Charles Beattie* as 1st Lieut. I am 1st Serg't.

James

H'd Quarters 14th Wis. Vol. Inf'y.
Eastport, Miss. Jan'y 13th 1865

Dear Mother:

The time has come at last when I can write something like a letter. We have been so continually on the move lately that I have had no time to write you more than a line for more than a month, but I hope that time has gone for good. I hope that I will have time after this to answer your letters as fast as rec'd.

Your last letter dated Dec 13th was rec'd on the 26th. When I wrote you those few lines from Clifton I didn't have time to answer the letter, so I put it off till we got into camp. . . . Now I wish I had some of the good butter you speak of. It seems as tho' I would relish it more just because it was made at home, & there's lots of other nice things that I miss having by not being at home, isn't there? Well I'll come home as soon as possible & have some of them.

I believe I told you something about the changes that have lately taken place in our Co. in my letter written from Clifton, but I didn't have time to write much, & so I will tell the whole story now. John Ryan was promoted to Capt. & Charles Beattie to 1st Lieut. on the 18th of last month. As soon as Johnny took command of the Co. he appointed the "Non-Commissioned Officers;" I was promoted to 1st Serg't . . . Lieut Wheeler might have been Capt but he declined promotion, so Ryan and Beattie "jumped" him. Wheeler expects to be mustered out some time this winter, but when, he does not know. Since I was Orderly I have had to do my regular duty & act as Co. Cl'k besides. Sometimes I have my hands full.

I have not given you any acc't yet of our travels since we left Nashville, so I will try to at this time. We left Nashville on the 15th & had a hand in the fight on that day, the next day we were in reserve & from where we lay in line I had a Splendid view of the charge made in the afternoon along the entire line. I never had such a good chance before to witness a battle, but I cannot describe it & do justice to the subject so I will not try.

The next day we started on after the enemy & followed them as far as Pulaski, Tenn. On the morning of the 24th Capt Fox [6] of Co "K" was mustered out & started for home. He offered to take any letters which we might want to send to Nashville & post them for us, so I improved the opportunity by sending word that I was alive & well. Whether you rec'd the line I wrote or not I have never heard.

From Pulaski our Corps took the road to Clifton on the Tenn. river leaving the 4th Corps to follow up Old Hood. We reached Clifton on the 2d of Jan'y, & camped there just long enough for me to make out the Muster rolls & write another line home which I hope you rec'd. We left Clifton on Sunday night & went on board a transport bound for this place which was reached on the 10th. "They say" we have gone into winter q'rs at last, but I'm afraid one of these Generals will take it into his head to issue an order cutting the winter short a month or two. If so we wont stay here long, but while we do stay I intend to do some letter writing if its possible to get Stamps. . . .

Give my love to *every body* especially *our folks,*

Your Dutiful Son

James

---

[6] Captain Ogden W. Fox of Baraboo.

Head Quarters *14th Wis. V.V.I.*
Eastport, Miss. Jany 26th 1865

Dear Mother:

I have seated myself this evening to answer a letter of yours written months ago, but rec'd about five days ago; where it has been all this long time I'm sure I cant tell; it is dated Nov 8th/64, but notwithstanding all that I found it very interesting. How many—many changes have taken place since then. It seems as tho' there was nothing but changes in this world, nothing that we see is to be depended on. And with us we never know in the morning, what sort of a situation we will be in before night overtakes us.

Since I wrote you last we have been on another "tramp." We went out to Corinth by the way of Iuka; the old place looked as natural as ever notwithstanding the peculiar circumstance under which I left it about two & a half years ago. We found the old "Tishamingo Hotel" in flames, probably set on fire by the Rebs who left the place on learning of our approach.

We had a pretty hard march, & especially the last day— it stormed all night before we got back to camp & all that day too, making the road very muddy & traveling hard. Since then the weather has been very cold, making it far from comfortable even in our log Shanties.

I see by the papers that all of Gen. Thomas' Army is well supplied with rations & every thing needful for their comfort. I wish their saying so would make it so, but unfortunately it does not: we are well supplied with clothing —in fact we have everything needful in that respect; but the fact is our "hard tack" has given out, & the troops here have been living on shelled corn for three days. We get meat & coffee besides, & that is all; however we get enough such as it is. You would not believe how many ways we can cook our corn so as to have a variety. We have parched corn, boiled Do. mush, corn coffee &c but the latest invention to make it *go down good* is to half parch it, & then grind it coarse like hominy & then boil it with a small piece of pork to season it. N.B. If you have to live on corn altogether, by reason of this war's continuing for a great length of time longer I advise you to cook it in the way I last mentioned.

I suppose you'll think it's pretty hard to live so, wonder how we can stand it, &c, but you would get over that if you could see how cheerful the boys bear up under their misfortunes. They take it all as a matter of course, & just because we draw corn for rations dont prevent their swearing at the Commissary if they think he gives any Co. more than their share, & they wont allow him to keep more than his share either. Well, we all know that we are better off than "our friends over the way" (the Rebs) for they draw their corn in the ear, & you see they have to shell it & we dont. When we drove them out of Columbia, Tenn., the citizens said that they issued five days rations to all the troops, five ears of corn to a man *with the husks on*—another difference in our favor. Well there's good times coming so we'll continue to live in hopes, & by the way thats the way a soldier always lives, in hopes that the morrow will bring something better. There is a fleet of boats on its way up the [river] which ought to have been here several days ago, when they get here we'll [have] plenty of rations. . . .

But I must close. Love to all & remember me ever
as Your Dutiful Son

Jas. K. Newton

H'd Q'rs 14th Wis. Vol. Infy
Eastport, Miss. January 31st 1865

My Dear Mother,

Your welcome letter of Jan 12th was rec'd today, & throwing everything to one side I have sat down to answer it. Our Brigade has gone out to Iuka. I would have gone myself but the payrolls had to be made out & I was left behind to work on them & for that reason I am able to answer your letter so promptly: the payrolls have to stand back you see. The Brigade went out after lumber to put up storehouses on the Levee. I expect they will get back tomorrow.

I had the pleasure of seeing Sam the other day. I heard they had got here on Saturday & on Sunday I started out to hunt him up. I found him on the other side of the river & had a good long talk with him. He seems to stand the service as well as could be expected considering the hard times he has been thro'. He has a couple of pretty sore fingers that he showed me; he froze them on that trip from Louisville, Ky, but for all the hard times he says he wouldn't be in the Infy for anything, & thats just where he & I differ.

When I got over there he was just eating his dinner—a plate full of mush with a piece of fried pork to make it go down easy. So you see he is used to high living as well as we are. He says they wouldn't issue rations of corn for the horses while hard bread was so scarce for fear the men would eat it all; so the horses were fed on oats. But all those hard times are ended, for we have plenty of rations now.

When I was over the river I told Sam if he could only come over some time I'd give him enough to eat for once, & he promised to come but has had no opportunity of doing so as yet. I hope to see him tomorrow tho'; if he was only on this [side] of the river 'twould be a great deal pleasanter to both of us.

As for me I have first rate health—with all their short rations I manage to get enough somehow or other. It fairly makes my mouth water tho to hear of all the good butter you are making & selling so cheap. Down here we have to pay from 85 c'ts to $1.00 per lb. & firkin butter at that. David Hawley bought some today for our mess for 85 c'ts & we thought it cheap. The Sutler sold his crackers for 40, 45, & 50 C'ts per lb while the rations were so scarce & then he sold all out in the first two days. Everything else here is in proportion very dear . . .

With love to all the family I am as ever

Your Affectionate Son

Jas. K. Newton

H'd Q'rs 14th Wis. Vol. Infy
Camp near Vicksburg, Miss.
Friday, Feb. 17/65

Dear Father:—

Your very welcome letter of Jan. 26th was rec'd yesterday, & now that we have got settled down in camp once more I'm going to try & answer it. I am still enjoying my usual good health, which even a ten days ride on a Steamer could not break up; tho' it left me with something of a cold to doctor on; but I managed to get hold of a bottle of "Ayers Cherry Pectoral" in Memphis, and now I'm about as good as new.

I'm afraid you worry about Samuel a great deal more than you would, could you have seen him as I saw him at

Eastport. I was afraid that he would be rather lowspirited & homesick, considering the manner in which he came into the service, but I found him anything but homesick: to use his own words he "had *nearly* time enough to turn round, three times during the day." When time passes off as fast as that to a Soldier, he hasn't time to be homesick.

Its true that Sam had the Diarrhea, but that is what every new Soldier has, but it operates differently on different persons. I would not give much for any persons life who has the diarrhea, & gives up entirely to the lowspirited feelings which he is sure to have at the same time. That is one reason why the mortality is not so great among Recruits who go into old Reg'ts, as among the new Reg'ts: the "Veterans" know how to take care of themselves, & the others profit by their example: as for homesickness a person dont get much sympathy who shows such a disease in a Veteran Reg't.

I had almost forgotten that we had moved since I wrote last: but our journey down the River was void of incident so I will say nothing about it. We reached this place on the 13th but did not leave the boat until yesterday morning. We expected to go on down the river. We are camped about 4 miles from Vicksburg in a very pleasant spot, & I for one wouldn't object to staying here six months. You know the war would go on just the same if we did stay here, so that wouldn't make any difference.

There is quite a handsome monument erected on the spot where Gen'l's Grant & Pemberton held that interview on the ever memorable—at least to us—3d of July 1863, previous to the surrender of Vicksburg. The tree that used to mark the spot when I was here last has been dug up root & branch & doubtless is now scattered all over the north, where the pieces are looked upon as great curiosities. The inscription on the monument is, "Site of the inter-

view between Maj. Gen. U. S. Grant & Lieut. Gen Pemberton C.S.A. July 3d 1863." . . .

    With love to all the family I remain as ever

Your Dutiful Son

Jas. K. Newton

Near New Orleans, La—

Wednesday March 1st 1865

Dear Father & Mother:

    . . . I am enjoying my usual good health, which by the
way, is uninterrupted now by cold weather. One would
hardly think that they knew anything about cold weather
down here. We had splendid weather on the trip down
here, but it commenced to rain the very day we reached
the Levee, & it has rained steady every day but one since
then. We are camped in an old cotton field about 7 miles
below the City & I'll leave you to imagine what a nice
camp we must have, stopping only to remark that the land
is perfectly level & below the level of the river, considerable.

    We are expecting marching orders every day, but as yet
we do not know where we are going. I *think* we are intended to operate against Mobile if it is found necessary
to send troops there. I begin to think that they'll get scared
& capitulate as soon as we *start for 'em.*

    What glorious news the papers are scattering abroad
nowadays! I only hope it may be true. The Gun boats have
to fire a salute every day in honor of some victory. Quite a
number of guns were fired this forenoon but I have not
heard yet what for. There is a rumor that Richmond is
evacuated. Maybe it has been confirmed. I wish you could

have heard the joyful shouts of the soldiers over the occupation of Charleston by our troops. I guess the Rebs
have begun their "concentration plan" in good earnest, &
Grant & Sherman are hurrying them up. If I am not won-
derfully mistaken all Grant wants is to have them concen-
trate their forces, for then they're "gone up," surely. . . .

I have been at work as fast as possible for 3 or 4 days on
the Muster Rolls, & as our "house" consists of a tent fly
open at both ends for the wind to blow thro' you can
imagine how much I could do. I could not write any nights
for the winds blows so all the time that I cannot have a
candle; that is the only reason why I have not written before. I had hoped, too, that by waiting I could get a letter
to answer, but I'm afraid now that we'll leave here before
my letters arrive.

Love to all the family & by all means dont forget to write
often. Write all the news.

Your affectionate Son

Jas. K. Newton

H'd Q'rs 14th Wis. Vol. Infy
Near New Orleans, La. Mar 5th 1865

Dear Mother,

Your welcome letter dated Feb 14th was rec'd last evening. I had begun to think that you had forgotten all
about "poor me" now that I had got so far down in this
heathenish country, but was convinced to the contrary on
reading your letter.

I dont wonder that you feel anxious about Samuel, but
really I think you need not worry on account of his not
writing, for you cannot imagine how difficult it is for him

to write even a few lines especially now that he is off on an active campaign. I think it will be very likely to be weeks & maybe months after they leave Eastport before he will even receive a letter from you let alone writing one, for you know the campaign this spring & summer is what is going to wind up this Rebellion, for that reason the preparations that are being made are on a grander scale than ever. The Cavalry that has been concentrated at Eastport were taken there for a purpose, & that a good one too. . . .

I sent an Over Coat & a Blanket by Express yesterday, but I dont think you will get them for a day or two after you do this letter. I sent them in a bundle to Mrs Wheeler along with some things that the Lieut sent home, you will get the things from her. You see it's getting warm weather down here now & our Great Coats & extra Blankets are just so much dead weight. I advise you to hang them out doors & maybe scald them, for there's no telling how many tenants they have. . . .

Respects to all enquiring friends.

I am as ever
Your Affectionate
Son

Jas. K. Newton

H'd Q'rs 14th Wis. Vol. Infy
Before Spanish Fort, Near Mobile, Ala.
Sunday April 2d 1865

Dear Mother:

I rec'd your welcome letter dated Mar. 9th day before yesterday. I was very glad to hear from you, but sorry to hear that there was so much sickness in the family. I hope that before this you have all recovered your usual health.

It is almost two years since I had to write under such circumstances as the present. We are right in the midst of a siege similar to that of Vicksburg, "only more so," & we have had to pass thro' a good many dangers: but now we are comparatively safe.

The first few days we had to work pretty hard for our own safety to say nothing of our operations against the Rebs: they threw shell in amongst us so much that it took all our time to dodge them, till finally we built a line of breastworks in front & traverses to protect our flanks & now we are having a breathing spell. I dont know whether you will get this letter very soon, but I hope so. The Steamers have effected a Landing on the left of our line & we are in no danger of running short of rations, but whether they will let a mail go out yet is more than I can tell.

From Dauphin Id. we went up the Bay to Fish R. & up the river to a place called Donnelleys Mills: from there we marched round to this place & I think we took them somewhat by surprise. They expected us up the other side of the Bay & in fact there was a Brigade sent to effect a landing at Dog River, but it was only a feint to cover our real purpose.

We reached this place on the 27th and now our left rests on the Bay & our right on the Tensaw R. The fort commands the channel between Dog R. Bar & the shore on this side & besides, the channel is lined with torpedoes.[7] That is the only reason that our Gunboats have not tried to run past the fort & bombard the city. The Gunboat men have been engaged for some time (& are now) in fishing them out, & so far they have been very successfull. Some of those taken out yesterday were common beer kegs filled with

[7] Torpedoes, in Civil War terms, meant what are now called mines.

powder & covered with resin to the depth of about two inches.

This morning I heard very heavy Artillery & musketry firing in the direction of Blakely & the supposition is that Steele is swinging round in the direction of Mobile. Quite a large train loaded with rations was sent to him from here day before yesterday. You know he started from Pensacola. When we first besieged the fort the Rebs had the advantage of us in heavy ordnance, but now there is no less than 16 30-pounders—Parrotts—in the front occupied by the 16th Corps beside nearly a dozen 10-inch mortars. We haven't got them all into position yet but I expect they will be in the morning, then we'll give them a lively time.

Our [Regiment] was out skirmishing the first day we got here, & we had a great old time dodging around in the abattis in front of the fort: we worked our way up until we drove all the Rebel skirmishers into the fort & then we had things all our own way. We fired so lively that they dare not show their heads over the works. We were so close that they could not depress their cannon enough to touch us & some of the boys in front of one of the portholes completely silenced the Gun it contained: nearly half of the cannoniers were negroes & I'm afraid some of them got hurt that day. We had one man wounded severely, he was shot thro' the right thigh but the bone was not broken & I think he will not lose his leg. . . . Our Reg't has lost nine killed & wounded: one man was killed yesterday in the rifle pits. The 33d Wis. has been particularly unfortunate, they have lost no less than 38 men killed & wounded.

Our Co. was detailed night before last to advance the skirmish line & we had quite a lively time, the Rebs fired on us & made some pretty good shots; fortunately none of us were wounded.

The Adj't. has just sent word that our Co. will go on the

skirmish line tonight & I must close for I've got to go &
draw the necessary ammunition.
    With love to all the family I remain
Your Affectionate Son

Jas. K. Newton

H'd Q'rs 14th Wis. Vol. Infy.
Before Spanish Fort, near Mobile, Ala.
Wednesday April 5th 1865

Dear Father & Mother:—
    . . . I was obliged to make my last letter shorter than I
wished on account of our Co. being detailed for skirmishers. We were not so fortunate the next day as some
of the Co's have been, for early the next morning one of
our Oneidas named Henry Hill was shot thro' the head &
I'm afraid mortally wounded: the bullet went in on the
left check & lodged over the right eye & tho' he is yet alive
I'm afraid he will never recover.
    The loss in our Regt up to this time is One killed, & Ten
wounded. Yesterday afternoon a general bombardment
took place all round the line, & we were all apprehensive
that a charge was going to be made: but our apprehensions
amounted to nothing that time. Since our illfated charge
on the fortifications at Vicksburg hardly a man in the Regt
can think of charging again without shuddering, & tho' we
would go if we were so ordered, it would not be with that
spirit & belief in our success, in which every charge should
be made.
    For my own part—& I believe I speak the mind of the
whole Regt—if it were on an open field I would say

charge at once for we can whip the Rebs every time at that game, & I believe too that it is a saving of life: but charging on fortifications with an almost impregnable abattis in front besides a ditch from 8 to 12 feet deep & as many wide is altogether a different matter. However I dont believe we have but one General here who would risk a charge— that one is Osterhaus [8]—I'm sure A. J. Smith—or Old Dad, as we call him—wouldn't. They have just made a detail for Sappers & Miners & that is another indication that the head ones intend to take the place by a regular siege. . . .

I dont think Sam's frozen fingers would prevent his writing, I'm sure it wouldn't, but there may be a dozen other reasons why he dont write. You know the 1st Cav. is with Thomas' army & lately we dont hear anything about where he is, or what he is doing. I dont believe Sam could send letters even if he should write them & I'm certain he hasn't any spare time to write moving around as they must be all the time: that is the greatest objection I have to the Cav. service. I dont know what I should do if it were not for writing & receiving letters.

Has Ed got his account with Gov. settled up yet? For fear he has not I will enclose a circular that was sent me from Madison a few days ago. . . .

But I must close. With love to all the family I remain as ever

Your Affectionate Son
Jas. K. Newton

---

[8] Major-General Peter J. Osterhaus, chief-of-staff of the Military Division of Western Mississippi.

> H'd Quarters 14th Wis. V.I.
> Spanish Fort, near Mobile, Ala.
> Sunday Morning, Apr. 9, 1865

Dear Father & Mother:—

Spanish Fort is ours at last! Last evening a charge was made by the 3d Brig. on our right which was entirely successful. It resulted in forcing back their left flank till we gained a position from which we could rake the enemy's breastworks. If they had only been driven a little further we would have captured the whole garrison: but the Gen'l seemed to think he had done well enough for one day, so he stopped to fortify & get ready to "give it to them" in the morning, but about midnight he found out they were leaving as fast as possible, so he pushed on & occupied the fort, capturing several hundred prisoners. The largest share of them got away on transports.

Where they are going is more than I can make out, for the report is that Steele has captured the forts at Blakely,[9] & if they go to Mobile we can soon drive them out of there. Thomas has captured Selma & Montgomery & is moving down from that direction, so there will be nothing for them to do but to give it up for a bad job. When we effect a

---

[9] Fort Blakely lay immediately to the north of Spanish Fort. Both forts were on the northeastern shore of Mobile Bay; the city itself was on the northwestern shore. At Spanish Fort the Union forces captured about 500 Confederates, while General Dabney H. Maury managed to escape with around 8,500 men. Steele, meanwhile, had been besieging Fort Blakely for more than a week; he captured it on the day Newton wrote this letter, April 9. During the total operations, including those of Steele, the Union loss was 189 killed, 1,201 wounded, and 27 captured—a total of 1,417. Including Steele's capture of Blakely, the total of Confederate prisoners taken amounted to 3,423. The two sieges virtually ended operations in the Gulf Coast region.

junction with Steele I hope to run across Sam'l. (I should have said Thomas, instead of Steele.)

We have a great joke on the 13th Corps; after our men had got inside the fort they mounted the breastworks & gave a cheer: the 13th Corps thought the Rebs were going to make a charge, & they began to fire at a great rate into our own men. They felt rather sheepish when they found out who they were firing at. The Gunboats too, threw one 11 inch shell into the fort after we had occupied it, but did no damage that I am aware of.

It is very likely we will move soon now, but where, or in what direction, I cannot tell. I thought I would scribble off these few lines so that you need not feel alarmed if I do not write [for] a week or so.

Really, dont you begin to see the "beginning of the end"? I do. By the way, the prisoners we have taken tell us that Petersburg has really fallen & probably Richmond too by this time.[10] They all seem to be heartily sick of the war; some of them go so far as to say that the principal portion of the inhabitants of Mobile are praying for our success. I doubt not their prayers will be answered & that very soon. It will be a happy day when the "war worn veterans" return to their homes, won't it? Just think of it! veterans of from 18 to 25 years.

But I have no time to write more, further than to assure you of my continued good health. That's all I thought I would be able to write when I commenced.

Love to all the family,

From Your Dutiful Son

Jas. K. Newton

---

[10] Petersburg, Virginia, fell on April 2; Richmond, on April 3.

H'd Q'rs 14" Wis. Vol. Infy
Near Montgomery, Ala. May 7" 1865

Dear Father & Mother:—

I hardly thought when I wrote you last from Spanish Fort that such a length of time would elapse before I would be able to write again, but so it is. I might have written before, but it would have done no good, for as yet the mail has not left this place. Our communications with the outer world have been entirely cut off until yesterday, just at the time of all others when we would most like to get the news regular.

The desire for news was so great that we were prepared to believe almost anything, but nevertheless the news of the assassination of President Lincoln & Seward was very sudden.[11] The flags are all flying at half mast today & half hour guns are being fired. There will be minutes guns fired from sunset until midnight. At the north I doubt not his death is felt to be a great national calamity, but nowhere is such sincere sorrow felt as here in the army. No man, not even Grant himself, possesses the entire love of the army as did President Lincoln. We mourn him not only as a President but as a man, for we had learned to love him as one possessed of every manly principle.

We reached here on the 25" inst[11a] & the next day our rations gave out: we expected to find the Gunboats & Transports here ahead of us with plenty of rations, but nothing was seen of them till last evening when they hove in sight down the river. We have been living on cornmeal & fresh beef, & we've got heartily sick of it too.

---

[11] Secretary of State William H. Seward was wounded by a knife stab, but recovered.

[11a] Although the letter reads "inst" Newton presumably meant to write "ult" to refer to the previous month.

As for my health it has been first rate all thro' this campaign, which I hope may prove to be the last campaign of the war. Oh! how I would like to see a late northern paper! as it is I know nothing whatever of the results of our late victories in the east,—but I earnestly hope that peace may result from them, that this army may soon be disbanded so that we can return to our happy homes once more.

I went down to the City yesterday & attended divine service in the Capitol where four years ago Jeff. Davis delivered his Inaugural Address. The room was crowded principally with soldiers, but I noticed a few citizens there & several ladies. The sermon was preached by one of our army Chaplains, & was really very good. The text was, "And they laughed him to scorn."—I'm not sufficiently well posted to give you the exact chapter & verse—He ennumerated the many ways in which God was laughed to scorn, & instanced the rebellion as one: he also spoke of the time "when in that very room the Solemn compact made by our fathers was laughed to scorn by the south, who boasted that it would be a holiday task to establish the southern confederacy." Take it altogether it was the best sermon I've listened to for a long time.

Gen. Steele came up on the boats with a division of Niggers & I hear that he has been appointed Mil. Gov. of Ala. If so we will not stay here long. If we go anywhere I hope it will be down to Mobile for there we will get paid, & stand a good chance to be mustered out of service among the first, as soon as peace is proclaimed.

We have a splendid camp ground here, the best one we were ever on. It is in a thick oak grove a little over three miles from the City—& if we are only allowed to stay here a little while I expect to have time to write some good long letters home after I finish the Muster & Pay Rolls. I was

hard at work on them when I heard that the mail would leave in a short time so I dropped everything to scribble off this letter. I must close this up now & go to work again.
Love to all the family
Your Affectionate Son
Jas. K. Newton

From Samuel Newton.

Macon, Ga. May 12th '65

Dear Parents.

I am agoing to write you a letter now that I have time and have it ready when the next mail goes out, which will be probably next week or as soon as the next dispatch goes through. I wrote you a few lines on the tenth to let you know that I am still alive and now I propose to tell you of a few things that I have seen.

After leaving the river we marched to Jasper. Here we first met their advance, they were only scouts sent out to see what we were doing and of course did not bother us much. Then we struck for Iron Ridge and began our work of distruction in their Iron Factories. We could see fires in every direction for three days. After marching several days our Brig'd struck out for Centerville, here our Co took the Advance. We went on a dead run for 18 miles capturing the vidette on his post, we then haulted and drew sabre and saluted the citizens as well as the soldiers with a grand old sabre charge and it was ours. Then our Battalion held the bridge untill the Division could come up and cross and burn the Factories in Edgefield. There, they ran onto Old Forrest but they succeeded in doing their work and retreated in good shape.

Our next mark was Selma, the road was a continued battle ground for more than forty miles, but the second & fourth division were ahead of us here, it was [a] very strongly fortified place. The city was surrounded by three lines of breastworks and out side of them was a line of sharpen'd posts set close together so as to prevent a charge and cannon in accordance. I believe that you put one division of us in there and we could hold it against the whole rebel army. They repulsed our men the first time but they rallied and tried it over again and gain'd the day.

It was a great manufactoring place, almost every other house was an Arsonal or something of the kind. We lay there a week and when we left the town looked as though it was all on fire. They kept the negroes to work all the time running shell into the river for fear of spoiling to much private property.

Then we made for Montgomery. The night (May [April] 12) before we went into it we camped about three miles from it. Our skirmishers had some pretty hard fighting about dark. The next morning we could see a large smoke coming out of the city when we got about one mile from it we met the *Mayor* coming out under a flag of truce with an unconditional surrender of the place. The rebs had burn'd every thing and taken what cannon they could and left during the night. We over-took them before noon however and then it was charge after charge day after day which I want you to understand is no easy work. We then went (our Brig'd) by the way of West Point (Ga), the rest of the Command going to Columbus Ga. The rebs hearing that we threatened C's run every thing up to West P and made ready for an attack at C's. We attacked the two places at the same time. Our Co. happened to be lucky enough to support the battery so that all I had to do was to sit and look on. We took the city with out any trouble but the Fort was rather gritty. They held us about an hour Gen Tyler [12] said that he never would surrender but as soon as he was killed the ft was our's. We had to build bridges and carry them up and place them across the ditch under fire for our skirmishers to cross on, but we lost comparatively few men, you probably know our loss better than I do for I know nothing.

Then you see we had the pleasure of burning the trains that had been sent from C's which was no small amount. We then burned the R-r bridge and got the locamotives onto the straight road and fired up the hind one and started them, the consequence was that they found the bottom of the Chattahoochee. We had not been gone from the place an hour before Forrest was in there, some how or other he followed up all such squad pretty close.

Then we started for this place but the other divisions from C's had got in ahead of us and it surrender'd with [out] firing a gun. If they had men enough in here we could not have done any thing with them it is a very strong place. I see there is a great many cannon here that has the U.S. mark on. . . .

Continued Sunday May 14th

. . . The First Batt got back last night from that scout after Jeff.[13] They feel pretty hard against the 4th Mich to think that they should trick them in the way they did. You see the two happened to meet at Doublin and pretty close to Jeff's heels and the Col of the 4th agreed to lay back and paytroll the river and let our boys advance. Not

---

[12] Confederate General Robert C. Tyler.
[13] Confederate President Jefferson Davis.

long after they left he (Col 4th) heard of his (Jeffs) where-
abouts so he takes a squad of his best horses and cuts across
lots and in that way got in ahead and haulted to rest. When
our boys came up they (4th) haulted them. Our advance
fell back, thinking of course that it was Jeff, to make
ready. Then they advanced again and the 4th fired into
them but if the 4th did get Jeff they got the worst of the
fight too. We lost two killed and three wounded, and they
lost 3 killed and 2 wounded, besides being drove quite a
distance. The way our boys found them out was by a couple
of prisoners that they took.

Well I will stop here hoping to both hear from you and
see you soon

Samuel Newton

Hd Qr's 14th Wis Vol. Infy.
Near Montgomery, Ala., May 17th 1865

My Dear Parents

. . . Of course you have heard all the news—what more
can I say, but we are prepared to believe anything. An
official dispatch came to Hd Qr's last night, saying that Jeff
Davis had been captured somewhere in Ga. by Wilson's
cavalry, so we are certain that we have the *head* as well as
the "Foote"[14] of the Rebellion now & all we have got to
do is to put a stop to the wiggling of the tail off in Texas.
Well we have fought in the "last ditch," & I hope we will
soon be allowed to go back to more peaceful pursuits: for
my part I'm perfectly satisfied to go home as soon as they
make up their minds to muster us out.

---

[14] Newton is referring to Henry S. Foote, Mississippi politician.

What seems to bother the most of us now is what we are going to do when we leave the service, for you know pay day wont come around then as it does now. We have been taken care of so long now that I hardly know how it will seem to have to look out entirely for myself. I hope tho' that I will be equal to the task. . . . We haven't any of us been paid for over six months & some of the boys have eight & ten months pay due. If we were only going to be mustered out, & going home with all our pay in our pockets I would like it better. I declare I never know what it was to be homesick till within the past few days. When I went into the service I made up my mind to "see the thing thro'," & now that it is wound up they cant discharge me a minute too soon. . . .

Gen. Beauregard (C.S.A. defunct) came into this city yesterday & gave himself up. I dont know yet what disposition has been made of him, but I hope they wont let him go as Sherman did Howell Cobb.[15] For my part I believe in making these head men among the secessionists suffer a little. Make them feel, if it is possible for such men to feel, that the United States is able to punish traitors as well as put down treason. Neither do I like to see the inclination manifested that I find in some northern papers, that of praising up some of these leading southern Gen'ls like Lee and Ewell.[16] It's not right. They should instead be denounced, & in the most bitter terms too. What if they have some good qualities? Should a devil be extolled for some good quality which he might happen to possess? & we all know that the abilities possessed by them, which should have been exercised on the right side, have instead been exercised in doing all the evil possible for the last four

---

[15] Beauregard was paroled. Howell S. Cobb, Georgia politician and Confederate general, had been captured at Macon on April 20.

[16] Generals Robert E. Lee and Richard S. Ewell.

years. Just because they have displayed so much ability makes their sin all the more damning in my eyes.

I think there's no danger but that they will get their deserts for Pres. Johnson has manifested his determination to have justice done in several instances. I wonder if he ever recollects the speech he made during the winter of '60 & '61 just before the breaking out of the Rebellion, in reply to one made by Jeff Davis. Twas in the Senate Chamber, I believe, shaking his fist in the face of Jeff Davis he said "if I were the Chief magistrate of these United States *I would hang you.*" Now that he is the Chief magistrate I've no doubt he will stick to his original determination, & *I hope he will* for if there ever was a man who had forfited *all* claims to life, that man is Jeff. Davis.[17]

The City is nearly cleaned of Secesh Soldiers now, but till within a few days past there was any amount of them coming in & going out. There were representatives of all the large armies, Lee's, Johnson's,[18] & Dick Taylor's, all of them making for home as fast as possible. Lots of them were on crutches. . . .

With love to all the family I remain

Your Affectionate Son
Jas. K. Newton

Head Qr's 14" Wis. V.V.I.
Near Montgomery, Ala., May 27th 1865

My Dear Mother:
I hope I'll have a chance to finish this letter but I cant tell. . . .

---

[17] Davis was imprisoned for two years but never brought to trial.
[18] General Joseph E. Johnston.

To tell the truth I am getting heartily sick of the service now that the war is over. I used to think that I could stand as much rest as any one, especially when we were on those long marches, but I've come to the conclusion that continual moving is all that would reconcile me to staying in the service, & I'm not certain even that would reconcile me to it, now that the war is over. I think four years— nearly—has qualified me to appreciate the comforts of a good home rather more than I used to.

What an experience the last few years has been! I would not take any amount of money & have the events which have transpired in that length of time blotted out from my memory. . . .

Braxton Bragg of the "little more grape" fame, & the pirate Semmes of "Alabama" [19] notoriety came into the city day before yesterday. They were sent to our Brig. H'd Qr's *under guard* by the officer of the Picket & reported to the Pro. Marshal, whereupon they expressed themselves very much dissatisfied with the disrespect shown persons of their distinguished rank. The Pro. M. "couldn't see it" so they didn't get any satisfaction out of him. . . .

There is a great deal of talk about keeping the Veteran Reg'ts some months longer than they do the rest. If so whatever vacancies occur in such Regts in the officers will undoubtedly be filled. However I have my doubts about our being kept much longer than other Regts. . . . I can hardly realize that the time is coming when Reviews, Inspections, Dress Parades, Drills &c. will be counted as

---

[19] General Braxton Bragg gained his "little more grape" fame when, during a battle of the Mexican War, he was asked to increase the output of his artillery in the faces of onrushing Mexicans. Admiral Raphael Semmes commanded the Confederate commerce-raider *Alabama.*

things of the past as far as I am concerned: what a joyful time it will be! . . .

Give my love to all the family. . . .

Your Dutiful Son

Jas. K. Newton

Evening:

. . . An official dispatch has just been rec'd at H'd Q'rs announcing the surrender of Kirby Smith [20] & his whole army. Not an organized rebel force in the whole country now.

Glorious! isn't it?

Yours Ever

James

---

[20] Confederate General E. Kirby Smith surrendered on May 26.

CHAPTER NINE

EARLY RECONSTRUCTION
IN ALABAMA

Head Quarters 14th Wis. Vet. Vol. Infy.
Near Montgomery Ala. June 17″ 1865

My Dear Mother:

. . . I am so glad that everything is going on so well on the farm; I was afraid that Pa would not be able to hire anybody to help him plant, & for that reason part of the land would have to lay idle; I am happy to hear that my fears proved groundless. What a satisfaction it must be to you to see all of those fruit trees in full bloom, to think that your labor & pains have not been in vain, but that you may yet enjoy their fruits. I know it is a great gratification to me that it is so. But what a difference there is between this place & up there! Here we had plums & berries of all descriptions a month ago. Blackberries cannot be sold at any price, hardly given away, & there are some as splendid looking ones as I ever saw. I dont think they taste as good as those I used to pick, tho', for there is a bitter taste about them that I dont like, it reminds me of Quinine. . . .

I have about given up being mustered out myself before next winter, for the many perplexing questions now being proposed to the European powers have all got to be disposed of, & satisfactorily, too, before the army will be reduced enough for us to begin to think of going home. I have no fears, however of our having a war with *any* of those European powers, for they all have too great a respect for the U.S. at this present time, & I think that now is just the time for the U.S. to make any demands, for indemnity or any thing else, while she has an army at hand to enforce her demands.

I shall like to hear of England's being made to make good all of the losses occasioned by the "men of war" built by her for the Rebs, & I'll not be much averse to using compulsion in the matter. What an army there could be raised on short notice for that purpose! there would be no need of resorting to the draft; why right down here in Ala. a dozen Reg'ts could be raised on short notice, & the men who went would fight, too. I believe it would be better too if those very same men could be called away & given some employment (Uncle Sam's $16 a month is as good as any.) that would keep them out of mischief until the country gets settled down once more: then let them come back & they would fall right in with the existing state of things, & become good citizens in a short time.

I think there is a good prospect of our staying here in Ala. as long as we are needed in the service; for we are not going to be needed in that "army of observation" that is now being sent to Texas,[1] & as there has got to be troops kept here, our chance for staying is good. . . .

---

[1] The "army of observation," under General Philip H. Sheridan, was sent to the Texas border as a threat to the French and their puppet ruler in Mexico, Maximilian.

The country people begin to come in with "garden sass" & the market looks quite lively during the fore part of the day. Prices are pretty high, generally, as is to be expected.

I *hope* you will consider this worth reading: I have nothing more to write & so must close. . . .

Your Affectionate Son

Jas. K. Newton

From a letter which James apparently wrote about July 5, 1865, to one of his sisters. A part of the letter is missing.

. . . I spent the poorest "Fourth" this year that I ever expect to spend. I must give you a description of the way I passed the day & leave you to judge whether I hadn't some reason to be *cross* (thats what Ryan called me) when I got back to camp.

In the first place the Regt was "fell in" at daylight & fired three rounds of blank cartridges. At 8 o'cl'k we fell in again & had a Brigade Review. After that every man went where he pleased. Ryan, Beattie & myself went down to the city to witness the performance which was to take place there, but 'twas nearly over before we got there.

The citizens & military formed a procession, marched thro' the streets, & out to a little grove where they were regaled with "music by the band" & speeches from prominent men: you know there is hardly a prominent man here in the south who has not been an active secessionist, & it was highly ludicrous to hear them bluster & blow about their "undying devotion to the Union," "living & dying under that good old flag," (pointing to the Stars & Stripes)

& "let the fires of patriotism burn upon the altars of our hearts to the end of all time," &c. &c. & all this from the mouths of men (I will not say it came from their hearts for I dont believe it.) who, but a few short weeks ago did not scruple to use every vile epithet they could think of to express the contempt they felt for the Gov. but especially for us "Lincoln hirelings," as they were pleased to term us. Verily, the assurance of some persons passeth all human understanding.

But to proceed. After this grand farce was ended the crowd dispersed & every one went "on his own hook." *Our crowd* (Ryan, Beattie & I) went out to the race course to see the races that were to come off, but after we got out there we found everyone drunk as fools, fighting, quarreling, & "raising Cain" generally, so we got into a carriage & came back to camp in disgust. Now dont you think I had reason to be cross? And now, for fear you'll leave this in disgust, I'll quit, hoping that when next you write you'll give me a description of your Fourth. Love to all the family.

Your Affectionate Brother

Jas. K. Newton

Montgomery, Ala.

July 27, 1865

My Dear Mother:

I rec'd your kind letter dated July 3d several days ago, but till now I have had no opportunity of answering it. The same mail that brought me your letter brought my commission as 2d Lieut. & since then I have been running

round trying to get mustered in; my efforts in that direction turned out successfull today so at last I can subscribe myself "Yours &c. Lieut J. K. Newton" quite an honor, isn't it? I dont know as I feel any better for it tho.
. . . I hope you wont stop writing again for fear we will get home before receiving your letters, for they will be sure to catch up to us at Milwaukee or wherever else we stop to be mustered out, & for my part I wouldn't run the risk of going so long without letters again for anything. Write as often as you can & you will only the more oblige me. Love to all the family.

Your affectionate Son

Jas. K. Newton

Montgomery, Ala.
Aug. 18th 1865

My Dear Parents;

I ought to have written you before this, but the time slips by somehow, and how, I am sure I cant tell; I'm sure however that I was never so sick of the service as I am now, and I dont expect to get over the disease until I get to be "my own man again." I wish I knew when that happy event was going to take place, but maybe its as well that I do not.

Every thing is going on quietly here at present: the troops are all gone except five or six Reg'ts, one of which is ours; and we dont expect to leave as long as troops are needed here at Monty. . . .

Three or four days ago I was detailed for "Special Commissioner for Administering the Amnesty Oath," with H'd Q'rs at Nixburg, Ala., and I was ordered to enter on my duties immediately; accordingly I reported myself for transportation to Nixburg—which is about forty miles north of here—when I found I could not go for a week or more; maybe not at all. However I'm having a pretty good time of it. Nothing to do but to go down town once a day and report myself.

Its quite a joke on the citizens up in my district, tho'. They wont be allowed to vote at the coming election without they have first taken the oath, and theres no chance for them to take the oath: rather a hard case, is it not? The authorities however, dont seem to care anything about whether I go, or not. They seem to think that their duty is done as soon as they detail the Commissioners and order them to proceed to business.

I shouldn't wonder if I had a good chance for adventure if I go, for I will be off by myself *forty miles from anybody*. I'll have to depend on my own muscle, together with a little revolver I managed to get hold of. I haven't much money, but what little I have I believe I'd fight for, rather than have it taken away by bushwhackers. . . .

I may not write again very soon if I go out to Nixburg, for there's no mail route yet open. I'll write tho' as soon as I get back. . . .

Your Affectionate Son

Jas. K. Newton

Montgomery, Ala.

Sunday Aug 20" 1865

My Dear Brother

I rec'd your unexpected but none the less acceptable letter dated July 31" yesterday. Its the first letter you've written me since I enlisted & therefore I intend to show a proper alacrity in answering it, hoping by so doing to keep up the correspondence.

If I supposed that you knew at the time you wrote that I was *an Officer,* I would feel my dignity insulted considerable, but I guess you had not heard of my promotion & so did not know that "The Sergt" had played out. . . .

I expect to leave the city in the morning for a few weeks. I have been appointed Special Commissioner for Administering the Amnesty Oath, & I leave tomorrow for my station—Nixburg Ala, about forty miles from here—to commence my work. I dont believe I'll find it very hard, but I cant tell yet. . . .

If I stay in the service all winter I intend to have easier times of it than I have had so far since I enlisted. I'll get on detached Service somewhere; at H'd Q'rs if possible. Thus far I've had to work like a dog the most of the time.

We are having pretty hot weather, & have been for some time; it wont last longer than this month I guess. . . .

Give my love to all the folks & tell Mercena & Minnie that I wrote last.

Your Affectionate Brother

Jas. K. Newton
"Lieut and Special Com.
for Administering
Amnesty Oath."

You needn't address me by that title tho'. only thats the way I have to sign Official Documents.

Montgomery, Ala., Aug 28" 1865

My Dear Parents:

I have been running all over creation today & on the whole I feel pretty tired, but I cannot let the evening slip by without writing you a few lines, & especially as I leave the city in the morning for an absence of some days again.

I came back to the city yesterday after some stationery & blanks for use in my office at Nixburg, Ala. I met with quite a little accident out there last Friday night: the house in which I had my office was set on fire & burned to the ground. I lost all my papers, records & everything that I had that had anything to do with my business: consequently I was obliged to come back to town & make good the loss. . . .

I haven't any idea when I shall be relieved from duty as "Special Commissioner" at Nixburg, but I hope to before long, so that I can get back to the Regt: I dont feel right at all off by myself, when I have always stayed with the Regt before. And then I cannot get any mail while I am away, & part of the time I cannot even write letters.

I shall try to write however as often as possible.

My health is first rate; it never was better. It seems to agree with me "mighty well" to eat my meals at a table, & sleep in a bed, &c. &c. I'm sure I *like* it a great deal better. I expect to hear soon that the 14th Wis. has started for the State, & when I do Im going to pick up my traps in a hurry. . . .

If I had time I'd like to give you a slight description of the people out in the country, but I cannot. I'll have all that to tell in the long winter evenings after I get home.

Love to all the family.

Your Dutifull Son

Jas. K. Newton

*Office of Special Commissioner
for Administering Amnesty Oath.
Nixburg, Ala., Sunday Sept 24"/65*

Dear Mother:

I intend to go to Montgomery tomorrow on business and thinking you would like to hear from me I have devoted the forenoon to writing you a letter; I do it, too, contrary to the advice of Mrs. Seaman (the lady with whom I am boarding) who says she knows I was brought up different from that, but if I dont write today I'm afraid I wont write at all. 'Tis true I have plenty of time weekdays to write, but then I dont have the office all to myself as I have now. If it was possible for me to send letters to Monty whenever I write them I should not leave you so much in the dark as to my movements. . . .

I expect to be relieved now shortly; in fact that is one reason why I am going to Monty tomorrow. I think that I can get relieved by making a Statement of the facts of the case. I have not done anything for nearly a week. The people have stopped coming in, and I have about made up my mind that they have all taken the Oath. If they haven't it is their own fault.

I would be in a nice fix if the Regt should be mustered out and start for Wis. leaving me down here, wouldn't I? That is the main reason why I am so anxious about being relieved. If it were not for that, I could *stay here* in the service for a six months yet.

I have the best kind of a boarding place, and I only have to pay $15.00 per month; for this country that is very cheap, and especially when I get the best kind of board. I went over to Rockford yesterday, which is about 8 miles from here, to see how the Sp. Com. got along over there. (He belongs to the same Regt.) I found him living on Bacon and "Greens" and cornbread and he has to pay the same for board that I do. He thought he was doing first rate, so I didn't enlighten him at all for fear he would be envious.

The family where I board consists of Mr. Seaman, his wife, brother, two children, and half a dozen Niggers. I couldn't wish to have a pleasanter home while I stay south, for they have any quantity of books and old papers, so that I do not lack for reading matter, and you know that is a great consideration with me. Mrs Seaman has a splendid education, and very often in looking over the old papers I come across articles that she has contributed. I think you will readily allow that companionship with such persons will not hurt a person, even tho' they are "Secesh to the backbone," and have an utter contempt for everything Yankee.

You must remember they dont call me a Yankee. I'm a Western man: and even when I tell them that I am a Yankee, and glory in being one, they wont hear of it at all. The people down here all make a difference between the western troops, and those of the east; it seems as tho' they have more of a respect for those of the west. . . .

Love to all the family.

Your Dutiful Son

Jas. K. Newton

Newton was mustered out on October 9, 1865, and returned to Wisconsin to enter school at Ripon Academy, Ripon, Wisconsin.

Ripon, Wisc.
Sunday, Jan. 21st, 1866

Dear Father & Mother:

I have been here nearly three weeks & have not written you yet. I'll see now, if I cant make amends for my neglect. I can assure you tho' that the neglect was not intentional; & really I dont know as I should call it neglect, for you know I came here to study, & study has just occupied my mind completely. . . .

I had no idea that my time would be so completely occupied as it is. I thought I should have time to write, at least, but day after day slips by without my hardly knowing it. I thought the time went off fast enough in the army, but this life beats army life "all hollow." To tell the truth I like it a great deal better too. I wish now, I could spend the same length of time at study, that I did in the army. I think I could make it of some use to me, dont you?

When I first went at studying, I could not make any headway at all. It seemed as tho' my memory would not serve me at all. I persevered, however, & now I am beginning to get along nicely. . . .

We get along first rate as far as eating is concerned. 'Tis true we have some corn hash once in a while, but that dont amount to anything. We always have "lots" of good bread & butter, & there's no danger of my starving on that. . . .

If I dont go to bed soon I wont want to get up at half past five tomorrow morning, & if I dont I'll neither get my lessons, nor my breakfast. That wouldn't pay at all for when a person misses a meal here, its dead loss, & a lesson is too for that matter.

Love to all . . .

I am, &c.,

Your Dutiful Son

Jas. K. Newton

ROSTER OF COMPANY F

INDEX

ROSTER OF COMPANY F
FOURTEENTH WISCONSIN VOLUNTEER INFANTRY

OFFICERS

Captains: Joseph G. Lawton, comm. Oct. 21, '61, res. Apr. 18, '62.

Samuel Harrison, comm. Aug. 4, '62, wounded, Oct. 3, '62, Corinth, died Oct. 20, '62, wounds.

Delos A. Ward, comm. Oct. 20, '62, wounded, Corinth and Vicksburg, res. July 22, '63.

John P. Ryan, comm. Dec. 9, '64, enl. Oct. 16, '61, captured, Corinth; wounded, Vicksburg; M.O. Oct. 9, '65.

First Lieutenants: George W. Bowers, comm. Oct. 21, '61, res. Apr. 26, '62.

James Camm, comm. Apr. 18, '62, enl. Oct. 5, '61, res. Sept. 14, '62.

Oscar Cooley, comm. Oct. 20, '62, wounded, Vicksburg; reduced to ranks by sentence, Gen. Ct. Mar., Feb. 1, '64, deserted Aug. 2, '64.

Charles Beattie, comm. Dec. 9, '64, wounded, Vicksburg, M.O. Oct. 9, '65.

Second Lieutenants: Reuben Wheeler, comm. Oct. 20, '62, enl. Sept. 25, '61, wounded, Vicksburg, M.O. June 13, '65.

James K. Newton, comm. July 1, '65, enl. Sept. 30, '61, captured, Corinth, M.O. Oct. 9, '65.

ENLISTED MEN

Alden, George B., enl. Jan. 20, '64, M.O. Oct. 9, '65.

Antoine, Abram, enl. Jan. 4, '64, died June 11, '64, Vicksburg, disease.

175

Archiquet, Aaron, enl. Jan. 2, '64, M.O. May 18, '65.
Archiquet, John, enl. Mar. 11, '64, M.O. Oct. 9, '65.
Archiquet, Solomon, enl. Sept. 8, '64, M.O. May 31, '65.
Avery, John C., enl. Oct. 8, '61, disch. Aug. 6, '62.

Baird, Thomas, enl. Apr. 19, '64, died June 16, '64, Big Shanty, Ga., disease.
Beattie, Robert, enl. Oct. 15, '61, disch. July 25, '62, disability.
Bergman, Joseph, enl. Dec. 18, '61, killed in action, May 22, '63, Vicksburg.
Besan, Alexander, enl. Jan. 19, '64, M.O., July 11, '65.
Boon, William, enl. Sept. 26, '61, deserted Nov. 10, '62.
Bradford, Thomas, enl. Jan. 25, '64, M.O. Oct. 9, '65.
Bread, Daniel, enl. Mar. 4, '64, wounded, Aug. 8, '64, Atlanta, disch. July 10, '65, disability.
Brighton, Richard, enl. Sept. 13, '61, M.O. Jan. 25, '65.
Brisque, Moses, enl. Sept. 13, '61, captured, Evansville, Ind., M.O. Oct. 9, '65.
Brisk, Mitchel, enl. Dec. 8, '63, M.O. Oct. 9, '65.

Cady, Henry, enl. Oct. 29, '61, wounded, Vicksburg, died July 1, '63, Milliken's Bend, La., wounds.
Carrow, Joseph, enl. Mar. 22, '64, M.O. Oct. 9, '65.
Casey, Maurice, enl. Oct. 3, '61, disch. Nov. 22, '63, disability.
Cavill, William, enl. Sept. 13, '61, wounded, Corinth, died June 24, '63, Jefferson Barracks, Mo., disease.
Chrisjohn, Daniel, enl. Mar. 11, '64, M.O. July 27, '65.
Clifton, George, enl. Dec. 17, '61, died June 14, '62, St. Louis.
Colburn, Oliver, enl. Feb. 11, '62, M.O. Jan. 29, '65.
Conlon, Henry, enl. Mar. 4, '64, M.O. Oct. 9, '65.
Creamer, James, enl. Feb. 22, '64, died July 27, '65, Montgomery, disease.
Cronk, Hudson, enl. Oct. 24, '61, wounded, Shiloh, disch. July 25, '62, wounds.
Cronk, Andrew, enl. Oct. 23, '61, disch. Apr. 29, '62, disability.

Danforth, Cobus, enl. Jan. 4, '64, died Aug. 24, '64, St. Charles, Ark.

Danforth, John, enl. Mar. 5, '64, M.O. Oct. 9, '65.

Dashner, Solomon, enl. Feb. 8, '64, M.O. Oct. 9, '65.

Daun, Jacob, enl. Nov. 6, '61, M.O. Oct. 9, '65.

Dean, John, enl. Feb. 23, '64, M.O. Oct. 9, '65.

Dean, David, enl. Dec. 17, '61, M.O. Oct. 9, '65.

Dezalia, Oliver, enl. Feb. 1, '64, M.O. Oct. 9, '65.

Doberstein, Frederick, enl. Feb. 16, '64, M.O. Oct. 9, '65.

Dollar, John, enl. Oct. 13, '61, wounded, Corinth, disch. Feb. 23, '63, wounds.

Doxtator, Jacob, enl. Mar. 4, '64, dishonorably disch. Oct. 9, '65.

Doxtator, Cornelius, enl. Feb. 23, '64, M.O. May 15, '65.

Doxtator, Paul, enl. Jan. 2, '64, M.O. Oct. 9, '65.

Doxtator, George, enl. Mar. 4, '64, M.O. Oct. 9, '65.

Duirr, Phillip, enl. Sept. 13, '61, disch. Dec. 11, '62, disability.

Dupri, Thomas, enl. Sept. 26, '61, disch. Oct. 15, '62, disability.

Fassett, Frederick, enl. Feb. 20, '64, M.O. Oct. 9, '63 [sic].

Ferris, Charles, enl. Oct. 21, '61, Musician, M.O. Oct. 9, '65.

Field, Isaac, enl. Dec. 17, '61, M.O. Oct. 9, '65.

Fish, Samuel, Jr., enl. Dec. 17, '61, disch. Apr. 29, '62, disability.

Fish, Samuel, enl. Oct. 20, '61, disch. Sept. 20, '62, by order.

Flanders, John, enl. Nov. 19, '61, deserted Oct. 20, '62.

Fuller, Henry, enl. Jan. 23, '64, M.O. Oct. 9, '65.

Garrow, Joseph, enl. Feb. 19, '62, died June 5, '63, Milliken's Bend, disease.

Gerard, George, enl. Oct. 26, '61, Musician, M.O. Oct. 9, '65.

Girardin, Theodore, enl. Jan. 20, '64, M.O. Oct. 9, '65.

Gireau, Edward, enl. Sept. 17, '61, M.O. Oct. 9, '65.

Hamilton, William, enl. Dec. 17, '61, wounded, Vicksburg, M.O. Oct. 9, '65.

Harrison, Henry, enl. Oct. 21, '61, disch. Aug. 15, '62, disability.

Harford, Amos, enl. Nov. 28, '63, M.O. Oct. 9, '65.

Hawley, David, enl. Sept. 23, '61, M.O. Oct. 9, '65.

Hayward, Samuel, enl. Oct. 14, '61, disch. Sept. 10, '62.

Hibbard, Andrew, enl. Dec. 28, '61, disch. Dec. 2, '62, disability.

Hibbard, Edmund, enl. Sept. 30, '61, M.O. Jan. 29, '65.

Hill, Henry, enl. Sept. 10, '64, wounded, Spanish Fort, died Apr. 8, '65, Spanish Fort, Ala., wounds.

Hill, Abram, enl. Mar. 4, '64, M.O. Oct. 9, '65.

Hill, David, enl. Mar. 4, '64, M.O. May 15, '65.

Hill, Lewis, enl. Mar. 4, '64, M.O. Oct. 9, '65.

Howard, James, enl. Sept. 22, '61, wounded, Shiloh, disch. July 8, '62, wounds.

Howard, Lorenzo, enl. Sept. 22, '61, disch. May 10, '62, disability.

James, Antoine, enl. Jan. 4, '64, M.O. Oct. 9, '65.

Jaradan, Louis, enl. Jan. 19, '64, M.O. Oct. 9, '65.

Johnson, Peter, enl. Jan. 4, '64, deserted Sept. 21, '64.

King, Levi, enl. Sept. 13, '61, disch. Dec. 3, '62, disability.

King, Nicholas, enl. Jan. 4, '64, M.O. May 15, '65.

King, Adam, enl. Jan. 4, '64, wounded, Spanish Fort, M.O. Oct. 9, '65.

King, Simon, enl. Apr. 29, '64, killed in action, July 22, '64, Atlanta Campaign.

La Count, Alexis, enl. Jan. 28, '64, died Oct. 15, '64, Atlanta, disease.

Lafond, John, enl. Mar. 18, '64, M.O. Oct. 9, '65.

Laundry, Andrew, enl. Sept. 13, '64, dishonorably disch. July 1, '65.

Laundry, Joseph, enl. Sept. 30, '61, wounded, Vicksburg, M.O. Oct. 9, '65.

Lawson, Henry, enl. Mar. 30, '64, M.O. Oct. 9, '65.

Lawrence, John, enl. Oct. 14, '61, wounded, Shiloh, M.O. Oct. 9, '65.

Leason, William, enl. Feb. 26, '64, disch. Mar. 24, '65, disability.

Lentz, John, drafted Dec. 28, '64, M.O. Oct. 9, '65.

Leque, Peter, enl. Feb. 16, '62, M.O. Oct. 9, '65.

Leroy, John, enl. Sept. 13, '61, wounded, Shiloh, killed in action, May 22, '63, Vicksburg.

Londra, Joseph, enl. Feb. 17, '62, dropped Aug. 18, '62.

Maccabees, John, enl. Feb. 1, '64, M.O. Oct. 9, '65.

Manason, Joseph, enl. Jan. 23, '64, M.O. Oct. 9, '65.

Martin, Patrick, enl. Oct. 22, '61, captured, Corinth, M.O. July 29, '65.

Mayville, Peter, enl. Feb. 23, '64, M.O. Oct. 9, '65.

McFarland, John, enl. Sept. 13, '62, wounded, Vicksburg, died June 18, '63, Milliken's Bend, wounds.

McLimans, John, enl. Oct. 8, '61, deserted Jan. 18, '63.

McNeal, Thomas, enl. Feb. 2, '64, died May 9, '64, New Albany, Ind.

Michaelis, Charles, enl. Dec. 6, '61, wounded, Tupelo, Miss., M.O. Oct. 9, '65.

Milquit, Gregory, enl. Oct. 22, '61, wounded, Shiloh, disch. Aug. 15, '62, disability, drafted Dec. 28, '64, M.O. Oct. 9, '65.

Montour, Gideon, enl. Jan. 25, '64, M.O. Oct. 9, '65.

Morrison, Samuel, enl. Sept. 23, '61, killed in action, Oct. 3, '62, Corinth.

Morrison, Salathiel, enl. Oct. 12, '61, died Apr. 31 [sic], '62, on Hospital Steamer, disease.

Munger, John, enl. Oct. 19, '61, killed in action, June 18, '63, Vicksburg.

Munger, Charles, enl. Feb. 8, '64, M.O. Oct. 9, '65.

Muir, Robert, enl. Jan. 3, '62, transferred to Co. A.

Murphy, Dennis, enl. Sept. 13, '61, wounded four times on Oct. 3, '62, Corinth, disch. Nov. 13, '62, disability.

Nimham, James, enl. Mar. 4, '64, died Feb. 9, '65, Keokuk, Iowa, disease.

Nimham, Antony, enl. Mar. 4, '64, M.O. Oct. 9, '65.

O'Connor, Thomas, enl. Oct. 10, '61, disch. Mar. 21, '64, by order.

O'Connor, James, enl. Oct. 31, '61, wounded, Vicksburg, M.O. July 29, '65.

O'Neil, Thomas, enl. Oct. 16, '61, M.O. Oct. 9, '65.

Parkhill, William, enl. Apr. 9, '64, M.O. May 11, '65.

Parsons, Alexander, enl. Sept. 29, '61, wounded, Corinth, disch. Mar. 14, '63, disability.

Peep, Henry, enl. Sept. 26, '61, M.O. Oct. 9, '65.

Phelps, Jeremiah, enl. Sept. 30, '61, died May 21, '62, Jefferson Barracks, Mo.

Powlas, Moses, enl. Dec. 14, '63, deserted Dec. 31, '64.

Powlas, Peter, 1st, enl. Jan. 4, '64, M.O. Oct. 9, '65.

Powlas, Peter, 2nd, enl. Mar. 4, '64, M.O. Oct. 9, '65.

Powlas, Anton, enl. Sept. 12, '64, M.O. July 18, '65.

Powlas, George, enl. Jan. 2, '64, M.O. Oct. 9, '65.

Pranto, William, enl. Feb. 1, '62, transferred to Co. E.

Punshon, John, enl. Jan. 29, '64, M.O. Oct. 9, '65.

Putnam, John, enl. Oct. 2, '61, killed in action, Apr. 7, '62, Shiloh.

Rabbidean, Edward, enl. Feb. 1, '64, M.O. Oct. 9, '65.

Rabbidean, Louis, enl. Jan. 28, '64, wounded, Atlanta Campaign, M.O. Oct. 9, '65.

Rabbidean, Antoine, enl. Feb. 14, '65, M.O. Oct. 9, '65.

Rawley, John, enl. Sept. 23, '61, wounded, Vicksburg, disch. July 10, '63, disability.

Reed, Chauncey, enl. Oct. 20, '61, promoted Capt. Co. B, 48th U.S.C.T., May 1, '63.

Rockwood, Daniel, enl. Oct. 15, '61, died June 19, '62, Jefferson Barracks, Mo., disease.

Roes, Frank, enl. Sept. 13, '61, M.O. Jan. 29, '65.

Ryan, Patrick, enl. Oct. 16, '61, disch. Aug. 6, '62.

Seymour, Francis, enl. Feb. 17, '62, disch. Jan. 23, '63, disability.

Silas, Abram, enl. Jan. 5, '64, M.O. Oct. 9, '65.

Silas, Isaac, enl. Jan. 5, '64, M.O. Oct. 9, '65.

Silver, Frank, enl. Oct. 8, '61, captured, Shiloh, transferred Feb. 15, '64.

Skenadore, Jacob, enl. Sept. 10, '64, M.O. June 1, '65.

Steward, John, enl. Sept. 30, '61, died Sept. 6, '63, De Pere, Wis., disease.

Stewart, Thomas, enl. Sept. 13, '61, M.O. Oct. 9, '65.

Steele, Thomas, enl. Nov. 7, '61, wounded, Vicksburg, M.O. Oct. 9, '65.

Stephens, Henry, enl. Mar. 4, '64, M.O. Oct. 9, '65.

Stewart, Winslow, enl. Jan. 1, '64, M.O. May 29, '65.

St. John, Sandford, enl. Dec. 2, '61, Musician.

St. Louis, Eli, enl. Feb. 8, '64, wounded, Atlanta, M.O. July 28, '65.

Stout, William, enl. Oct. 16, '61, killed in action, May 22, '63, Vicksburg.

Sullivan, John, enl. Dec. 17, '61, wounded, Vicksburg, M.O. Jan. 29, '65.

Talcott, Jesse, enl. Oct. 15, '61, wounded, Vicksburg and Brownsville, Ark., M.O. Oct. 9, '65.

Thetro, Hamilton, enl. Sept. 15, '61, wounded, Vicksburg, M.O. Oct. 9, '65.

Thomas, Thomas, enl. Jan. 5, '64, died Oct. 4, '64, Brownsville Station, Ark.

Tidd, Alexander, enl. Sept. 30, '61, died Sept. 30, '62, Keokuk, Iowa.

Tilliman, John, enl. Sept. 26, '61, killed in action, May 22, '63, Vicksburg.

Turiff, Robert, enl. Feb. 19, '64, M.O. Oct. 9, '65.

Turiff, Thomas, enl. Sept. 13, '61, wounded, Vicksburg, M.O. Oct. 9, '65.

Valien, Israel, enl. Jan. 18, '64, M.O. Oct. 9, '65.

Verts, Andrew, enl. Feb. 16, '62, died July 26, '62, Hamburg, Tenn., disease.

Verts, David, enl. Feb. 28, '62, M.O. Feb. 21, '65.

Viean, Amos, enl. Feb. 1, '64, died May 10, '64, Pulaski, Tenn., disease.

Vincent, Charles, enl. Sept. 13, '61, wounded, Shiloh, disch. July 8, '62, wounds.

Waggoner, Abraham, enl. Feb. 17, '64, M.O. July 22, '65.

Webster, Augustus, enl. Apr. 20, '64, M.O. Oct. 9, '65.

Webster, Edgar, enl. Feb. 22, '64, M.O. Oct. 9, '65.

Webster, Lewis, enl. Jan. 1, '64, M.O. Oct. 9, '65.

Welch, John, enl. Jan. 28, '64, disch. Mar. 25, '65, disability.

Westcott, Daniel, enl. Oct. 15, '61, disch. Sept. 13, '62, disability.

Westcott, Henry, enl. Sept. 28, '61, wounded, Shiloh, disch. Dec. 9, '62, disability.

Westcott, Madison, enl. Sept. 23, '61, wounded, Vicksburg, M.O. Oct. 9, '65.

Wilson, John, enl. Feb. 9, '64, transferred to Co. E.

Woodward, George, enl. Sept. 26, '61, M.O. Oct. 9, '65.

Woodworth, George, enl. Nov. 28, '63, deserted Dec. 31, '64.

Wright, William, enl. Dec. 19, '61, wounded, Vicksburg, disch. July 17, '65, disability.

Zoeller, Alois, enl. Dec. 18, '61, M.O. Oct. 9, '65.

(Abbreviations: comm. for commissioned; enl. for enlisted; disch. for discharged; M.O. for mustered out; res. for resigned.)

This roster is taken from *Roster of Wisconsin Volunteers, War of the Rebellion, 1861–1865*, I, 787–90.